ANNUALS &
BIENNIALS

RICHARD ROSENFELD

A DORLING KINDERSLEY BOOK

DK

LONDON, NEW YORK, MUNICH, MELBOURNE, DELHI

Series Editor Zia Allaway
Series Art Editor Alison Donovan
Art Editor Ann Thompson
Editor Victoria Willan
Managing Editor Anna Kruger
Managing Art Editor Lee Griffiths
Consultant Louise Abbott
DTP Designer Louise Waller
Media Resources Richard Dabb, Lucy Claxton
Picture Research Bridget Tily
Production Controller Mandy Inness

Introduction text Zia Allaway

First published in Great Britain in 2003 by
Dorling Kindersley Limited
80 Strand, London, WC2R ORL
A Penguin company

A CIP catalogue record for this book is available
from The British Library
ISBN 0 7513 3821 4

Colour reproduction by Colourscan, Singapore
Printed and bound by Printer Trento, Italy

see our complete catalogue at
www.dk.com

Gardening with annuals and biennials

PICTURE A SUMMER'S DAY — a sea of flowers bathed in sunlight, butterflies flitting from bloom to bloom, sweet perfume wafting on a warm breeze. A dream-like image, perhaps, but one that can easily become reality with just a handful of seeds and a patch of bare earth. For that is all you need to create a garden filled with flowers, and by sowing annuals in spring you can achieve your personal paradise within just a few weeks. Biennials take a little longer to come into bloom, but their beauty and variety makes them well worth the wait.

Annuals are plants that germinate, grow and die within one year. Most produce a huge number of flowers in one season, resulting in lots of seeds that help to guarantee new plants the following year. Hardy annuals are the easiest to grow and can be sown outside from early spring in the place you want them to flower. Half hardy and tender varieties should be sown at the same time or slightly earlier, but in a frost-free environment, such as a greenhouse or on a sunny windowsill.

Biennials take two years to complete their life cycle. In the first year they produce leaves and establish a root system, and then they flower, set seed and finally die in the following year. Like annuals, they produce copious seeds that grow into

◀ **A garden of soft and delicate** small white daisies, set against pastel blues and pinks, offers the perfect antidote to a stressful day.

▶ **Deep purple campanulas** are among the most beautiful of the biennials.

Wild gardens filled with flowers include choice annuals and biennials that attract butterflies and bees.

new plants the following year. Many biennials self-seed freely and the resulting seedlings can be lifted and grown on in a separate area of the garden until they're ready to flower.

Using annuals and biennials

Annuals and biennials have infinite uses. A summer patio display would be incomplete without pots and hanging baskets packed with petunias, busy Lizzies (*Impatiens*) and trailing lobelia. Combine these colourful basket plants with scented annuals, such as stocks (*Matthiola*) and tobacco plants (*Nicotiana*), which can be planted in pots close to the house or seating areas. Annuals and biennials are equally

impressive in beds and borders where their continuous performance throughout the summer is hard to beat, and their diversity provides scope for all garden settings.

Formal bedding schemes can be mapped out in neat rows or patterns drawn with golden marigolds, pelargoniums, salvias and snap dragons (*Antirrhinum*). Informal gardens planted *en masse* with grasses, poppies, love-in-a-mist and cornflowers create a naturalistic scene, reminiscent of fields of wild flowers. Annuals and biennials can also contribute to wildlife gardens: the poached egg plant (*Limnanthes*) and calendulas attract bees and other beneficial insects, while the seeds of teasels (*Dipsacus*) prove irresistible to goldfinches.

Foliage effects

Although annuals and biennials are most commonly used for their flower effects, foliage

Colour enthusiasts appreciate the splendour of beds and borders brimming with flamboyant annuals.

Dazzling displays in the depths of winter are possible with colourful pansies or cheerful violas.

plants can also be found in these groups. The beautiful hand-shaped, deep purple-red leaves of the caster oil plant (*Ricinis communis*) add an architectural element to an exotic-style garden, and the aptly-named flame nettles (*Solenostemon*) will set planting schemes ablaze with their sizzling foliage.

These transient plants are useful, too, for filling gaps in mixed borders, especially where young perennials and shrubs are putting down roots but are yet to fill their allotted spaces.

Winter warmers

Although late spring to early autumn is the peak period for

Leafy baskets
Variegated nasturtiums and flame nettles pack a punch.

annuals and biennials, a smaller selection can continue the show right through the year. Violas and winter pansies, if kept on a sheltered patio, will flower throughout winter, and from early spring biennial wallflowers (*Erysimum cheiri*) burst into bloom, filling the air with their wonderful fragrance.

As if these gifts were not enough, the flowers of many varieties can be dried and used in floral arrangements. Statice (*Limonium sinuatum*), love-in-a-mist, and hare's tails (*Lagurus ovatus*) combine colour, shape and texture to form an everlasting display for the home.

Pots of primroses in hot shades will bring much needed colour on chilly days in early spring.

This book provides a quick reference to 300 of the best annuals and biennials. Some can be bought in spring as young plants, others are available as seeds from nurseries, garden centres or mail order specialists, and all guarantee a garden or patio bursting with flowers.

Annuals from seed

A LIVELY LOOKING BUNCH, annuals are easy to grow and many flower from seed within weeks of sowing, making them ideal for impatient gardeners keen to experiment with colour, texture and form. Hardy annuals can be sown outdoors *in situ* in spring, but half-hardy and tender types are best sown under cover, the seedlings planted out after the frosts.

Sowing hardy annuals in drills in borders

To get a good idea of just how well heights and colours will work together, it's useful to make a rough positional plan. Then sow your seeds in straight lines, or drills, which makes it easier to distinguish between the seedlings and weeds when they appear. Water drills before sowing.

1 Marking out
Use sand to mark out sections for different annuals. Loose arcs give a more informal or naturalistic look.

2 Sowing seeds
Trickle seeds evenly and thinly from your hand (fine seeds can be mixed with sand) into the drills.

3 Covering seeds
Gently brush soil across the drills, firm it down, and water it with a fine rose to avoid seed disturbance.

4 Thinning seedlings
Carefully pull out unwanted seedlings, leaving at least 5–6cm (2–2½in) between those remaining.

Sowing half-hardy annuals

You don't need a temperature controlled greenhouse to grow half-hardy or tender annuals, as most will be perfectly happy growing on a warm windowsill. First, avoid contamination from pests and diseases by soaking trays and pots in baby bottle sterilizer, or a similar disinfectant.

Sow your seeds in good quality seed compost, cover the trays with plastic film or glass (remove as soon as the seedlings start to emerge), and keep them indoors in a bright spot, but out of direct sun. When the seedlings appear, turn the trays daily to prevent spindly, lopsided growth.

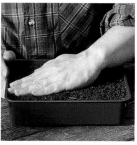

1 Firming the compost
Fill a tray with compost and then firm gently with another tray, your hand, or a wooden presser to about 1cm (½in) below the rim. Water the compost well and allow to drain.

2 Sowing seeds thinly
Cover the surface of the compost with a thin layer of seeds. Check the seed packet for the correct planting depth, and remember that most tiny seeds need light to germinate

3 Covering the tray
To keep the compost moist, cover the tray with plastic film or glass. Put the seeds in a light place, but not in full sun, and uncover the tray as soon as the seeds germinate.

Seeds sown into pots

If you only want a few plants, sow the seeds in small clay, biodegradable or plastic pots, using the same method as you would for trays. Don't over-firm the compost and take care not to overcrowd the seeds, as this can result in tall, spindly seedlings that are prone to fungal infections.

Using vermiculite
Vermiculite looks a bit like polystyrene and is good for covering seeds that need light to germinate. It helps to hold moisture and allows air to circulate around the seeds, reducing the risk of damping-off disease.

Pricking out and growing on

Once germinated, seedlings need bright light and moisture. Left in their trays too long, the seedlings soon become overcrowded, resulting in weak, spindly growth. To avoid this, transplant them when they have one or two true leaves (these develop after the first two leaves, which are seed leaves). Keep the seedlings well watered, using a fine spray to prevent soil disturbance.

1 Lifting seedlings
Use a widger or a pencil to carefully loosen the compost around seedlings before lifting them by their true leaves.

2 Replanting seedlings
Fill a tray with fresh compost and replant the seedlings, spacing them evenly. Water them in with a fine spray.

Pricking out into modules

Transplanting young seedlings into polystyrene or plastic module trays means that each seed can develop within its own space until it's ready to be potted up or planted out, thereby minimizing root disturbance. Modules need to be watered frequently as they tend to dry out quickly.

1 Lifting seedlings
Rather than removing seedlings one by one from trays, gently tip out the compost and work each one free from the edge. Be careful not to damage stems or fine roots.

2 Transplanting seedlings
Make a large hole in the centre of a module, plant the seedling and firm the compost around it. Water in well.

Growing hardy biennials

BIENNIALS ARE AMONG THE prettiest plants but only flower in their second year – when they set seed, bloom and die – and spend the first year developing leaves and roots. The seeds can be sown from early spring to summer, ideally in a separate bed where the seedlings have space to grow without any competition from other plants for light and water.

1 Lifting seedlings
By early summer, seedlings sown in spring should be 5–8cm (2–3in) tall, and can be lifted from the seedbed using a hand fork. Retain plenty of soil around the roots.

2 Planting out seedlings
Plant out your lifted seedlings at 15–20cm (6–8in) intervals in a nursery bed (allow the roots plenty of room) and firm them in gently before watering thoroughly.

3 Transferring seedlings
Lift your young plants and transfer them to their final spot in autumn. If the nursery bed is dry, give it a good water several hours before digging up the plants.

4 Overwintering biennials
Most biennials remain evergreen in winter, but a few wither back to a bud. Some hate excessive winter wet and should be protected by a plastic or glass cloche.

Collecting your own seed

THERE'S SOMETHING VERY SATISFYING about collecting seeds from your own plants, sowing them and watching them grow. The seeds of many annuals and biennials come true to type and produce flowers identical to the parents, but F1 hybrids and some cultivars don't, and their seeds will produce inferior plants. Buy fresh seeds of these varieties each year.

Removing seeds from capsules

It's best to collect seed capsules on a dry day, as seeds will rot if they're damp when stored. Split the capsules open over a piece of paper to catch all of the contents.

Collecting from the plant

Some ripened seeds can be collected straight from the plant. Simply pull them through your hand to sift seed and chaff into a plastic or paper bag.

Sorting seeds from chaff

Use a sieve to remove unwanted chaff from the seeds. Experiment with different mesh sizes so that only the seeds fall through, leaving unwanted chaff in the sieve.

Storing seeds

Store cleaned seed in a cool, dry place, away from bright light. An airtight plastic film canister, clearly labelled and kept on a shelf in the refrigerator, would be ideal.

Looking after annuals and biennials

FOR HEALTHY PLANTS, ensure your young annuals and biennials are well looked after. Protection against pests and diseases is vital for all plants, as is regular weeding and watering, especially for those in containers. Container-grown annuals and biennials must also be fed with a slow-release fertilizer or liquid feed, but those in beds or borders rarely need extra food, unless the soil is very poor.

▲ Hardening off young seedlings
In spring, harden off seedlings grown under cover. For a few weeks before the last frosts, place them outside during the day and bring them back inside at night.

◄ Providing support for young seedlings
The ideal supports for young annuals, twiggy sticks must be pushed into the soil with care to avoid root damage.

Deadheading ►
Regular deadheading removes ugly, fading flowers from plants. It also prolongs the flowering season of annuals and biennials by encouraging more blooms to develop. Pinch off the flower stem just above a leaf joint or bud.

Watering annuals ►
Annuals potted in soilless compost are best watered from below, especially when the compost is very dry. Place the pots in a bowl of water until the compost on the surface feels moist.

A–Z of Annuals and Biennials

A | *Abelmoschus moschatus* Pacific Range Musk mallow

THE HIBISCUS-LIKE FLOWERS of this bushy Indian annual are
5–7.5cm (2–3in) wide and usually pink ('Pacific Light Pink') or
scarlet ('Pacific Orange Scarlet') – a flower lasts one day, but others
keep on opening to provide a prolific supply. The musky-scented
seed capsules measure up to 7.5cm (3in) long and give the plant its
common name. The parent plant, *A. moschatus*, grows much taller, to
about 1.5m (5ft). Its leaves are up to 45cm (18in) long and the
flowers are typically yellow with a purple centre. Sow the seeds in
late winter or early spring under glass, or in mid-spring where they
are to grow, making sure that the soil is fertile and free-draining.

OTHER VARIETY *A. manihot* (yellow flowers with purple centres).

PLANT PROFILE

HEIGHT 40cm (16in)

SPREAD 40cm (16in)

SITE Full sun

SOIL Fertile, free-draining

HARDINESS Min. 5°C
(41°F)

FLOWERING Midsummer
to autumn

Abutilon Bella Hybrids **Flowering maple**

A

DEVELOPED IN COSTA RICA by the great plantsman Claude Hope, Bella Hybrids (not to be confused with the older Belle Series) are beautifully compact and dwarf, which makes them perfect for pots and windowboxes. The bell-shaped flowers emerge continuously in a wide range of delicate pastel shades, including soft apricot, pink, and yellow, and are about 8cm (3in) wide. Pot up the best plants in autumn and keep them in a conservatory for the winter. You can then put them out again the following summer. Sow the seeds in spring under glass, and grow on in fertile, moist soil.

OTHER VARIETY 'Large Flowered Mixed' (yellow, amber, apricot, crimson, and pink flowers).

PLANT PROFILE	
HEIGHT 40cm (16in)	
SPREAD 40cm (16in)	
SITE Partial sun	
SOIL Fertile, moist	
HARDINESS Half hardy	
FLOWERING Summer to early autumn	

A | *Acinos arvensis* Basil thyme

THE DELICATE SCENT of this short-lived, hardy perennial is faintly reminiscent of thyme (it's known as mother of thyme, as well as basil thyme), although it's better planted in a rock garden, as edging for a path, or at the front of a border than in a herb garden. Its significant features are its violet flowers with a white mark on the lower lip, and its spreading, downy, branching stems which make excellent ground cover. Sow the seeds in spring or autumn in a cold frame, and grow on in poor to average, free-draining soil.

PLANT PROFILE

HEIGHT 20cm (8in)

SPREAD 30cm (12in)

SITE Full sun

SOIL Poor to average, free-draining

HARDINESS Fully hardy

FLOWERING Mid- and late summer

Adonis aestivalis

A VERY ATTRACTIVE ANNUAL with feathery foliage and bright red flowers with a dark eye, *A. aestivalis* livens up wildflower gardens. In its native habitat, from France and Spain to Syria and Iran, it grows in rough ground. In cooler, north-west Europe it needs free-draining, average soil, leaning more to the poor than the rich. Since it is totally hardy you can sow the seeds where they are to flower in the autumn or following spring. Take precautions against slugs when the seedlings appear.

PLANT PROFILE
HEIGHT 40cm (16in)
SPREAD 30cm (12in)
SITE Full sun
SOIL Average, free-draining, alkaline
HARDINESS Fully hardy
FLOWERING Midsummer

A | *Adonis annua* Pheasant's eye

ORIGINALLY FROM SOUTHERN PARTS OF EUROPE and south-west
Asia, pheasant's eye adds a colourful and upright touch to the
cottage gardens of north-west Europe. Its small, cup-shaped, early
summer flowers are scarlet with a dark centre and about 2.5cm (1in)
wide. These are set off by finely divided, feathery foliage. As with *A.
aestivalis*, be especially vigilant for marauding slugs. Sow the seeds
where the plants are to flower in autumn or spring, and grow in
free-draining, average soil.

PLANT PROFILE

HEIGHT 45cm (18in)

SPREAD 30cm (12in)

SITE Full sun

SOIL Average, free-draining, alkaline

HARDINESS Fully hardy

FLOWERING Early summer

Ageratum houstonianum 'Adriatic' Floss flower

MEXICAN AGERATUMS, WITH THEIR COMPACT, mound-forming cultivars, flower in a range of extremely useful blues, and occasionally in white or pink (all self-seed). Heights range from just above the ankle to 45cm (18in) – 'Adriatic' is one of the shorter forms. This cultivar's flowers are small and fluffy, giving a hazy, fuzzy look, and sit on top of the leaves where they attract bees and butterflies. Keep watering 'Adriatic' in dry spells or flower production will slow down. Sow the seeds in autumn or spring under glass, and grow in fertile, moist but free-draining soil in a sheltered site.

OTHER VARIETY 'Bavaria' (blue-and-white flowers).

PLANT PROFILE

HEIGHT 20cm (8in)

SPREAD 20cm (8in)

SITE Full sun

SOIL Fertile, moist but free-draining

HARDINESS Half hardy

FLOWERING Midsummer to late autumn

A

Ageratum houstonianum 'Swing Pink' **Floss flower**

SHORT, COMPACT AND FREE FLOWERING, floss flowers are excellent for wall pots, hanging baskets and patio containers. These diminutive plants are also suited to edging, where they will not flop or nudge across paths – and this is where the fluffy, rounded heads of 'Swing Pink', which are produced in brush-like clusters right through the summer, look particularly effective. Sow the seeds in early spring under glass, and grow in fertile, moist but free-draining soil.

OTHER VARIETY Hawaii Series (uniform and compact, with deep to pale blue and white flowerheads).

PLANT PROFILE
HEIGHT 20cm (8in)
SPREAD 20cm (8in)
SITE Full sun
SOIL Fertile, moist but free-draining
HARDINESS Half hardy
FLOWERING Midsummer to late autumn

Agrostemma githago 'Milas' Corn cockle

A

THE CORN COCKLE MAKES WONDERFUL DRIFTS of bee-attracting flowers in borders or wild gardens. A cottage-garden favourite, it also makes an excellent cut flower. 'Milas', named after the Turkish town where it was found growing wild, produces rich pink flowers with a whitish centre and characteristically slender, silvery stems. It is the most popular and easily available of several forms, with 'Purple Queen' coming a close second. Sow the seeds in spring where they are to grow, or in autumn under glass for a tall pot plant the following summer. Grow 'Milas' in poor, light, free-draining soil.

OTHER VARIETY 'Ocean Pearl' (white flowers with black speckles).

PLANT PROFILE
HEIGHT 90cm (36in)
SPREAD 30cm (12in)
SITE Full sun
SOIL Poor, free-draining
HARDINESS Fully hardy
FLOWERING Summer

A | *Agrostis nebulosa* Cloud grass

WITH ITS LARGE, DELICATE HEADS – its tiny white spikelets emerge in clusters along the stem – cloud grass is definitely a favourite with flower arrangers. Grow it with other annual grasses, such as *Briza media* (common quaking grass) and *Lagurus ovatus* (hare's tail grass), or beside *Aira elegantissima* (hair grass) and *Panicum capillare* (witch grass) to build up a cloud-like show. Sow cloud grass seeds in spring where they are to grow; it is not fussy about the soil but will do best in a sunny spot.

PLANT PROFILE

HEIGHT 35cm (14in)

SPREAD 35cm (14in)

SITE Full sun

SOIL Almost any

HARDINESS Fully hardy

FLOWERING Late spring to midsummer

Alceas are good subjects for seed collection. The large seeds are plentiful and easy to handle – collect them as they ripen and sow in summer.

Alcea rosea Chater's Double Group Hollyhock

A

WITH THEIR STATELY SPIRES of cup-like flowers, hollyhocks are a superb sight. These short-lived perennials are traditionally grown in cottage gardens (stake in windy sites), where they attract bees and butterflies. Susceptible to rust (a fungal disease), they are often grown as annuals or biennials to prevent the build up of this problem. Chater's Double Group offers a wide range of colours, including pink, apricot, red, white, lavender-blue, yellow, and purple. Sow seeds in pots in midsummer in a greenhouse, or in winter on a windowsill in a cool room. To prevent rust, remove the leaves of mature plants in winter, and spray with fungicide in spring.

OTHER VARIETY 'Indian Spring' (white, pink or yellow flowers).

PLANT PROFILE
HEIGHT 2.5m (8ft)
SPREAD 60cm (24in)
SITE Full sun
SOIL Average, free-draining
HARDINESS Fully hardy
FLOWERING Early and midsummer

A | *Alcea rosea* 'Nigra' Hollyhock

FOR A RICH CONTRAST, wherever there is a group of pastel or red hollyhocks, include a few 'Nigra'. Its dramatic flowers, which look almost black from a distance, are ranged up the flower stem and face outwards like round saucers. To produce big plants, sow the seeds in midsummer and keep them in a greenhouse, or sow them on a windowsill over winter. Hollyhocks are susceptible to rust disease but you can minimize the damage by removing all the leaves in winter and spraying the plant with a fungicide in spring. Grow in average, free-draining soil.

OTHER VARIETIES Majorette Group (dwarf and bushy); 'Summer Carnival' (colours include pale yellow, and red).

PLANT PROFILE	
HEIGHT 2m (6ft)	
SPREAD 30cm (12in)	
SITE Full sun	
SOIL Average, free-draining	
HARDINESS Fully hardy	
FLOWERING Summer	

Alonsoa meridionalis Mask flower

THE STRIKING RED AND YELLOW FLOWERS of the mask flower are just right for a hot-coloured border. So tender is this multi-branching, bushy perennial that it is invariably grown as an annual. Snap up plants or seeds the moment you see them because mask flowers are difficult to find. Sow the seeds in early spring under glass for planting out after the last frost, and grow in fertile, free-draining soil. Thereafter, take cuttings in early autumn and overwinter indoors; plant out in summer.

OTHER VARIETY Firestone Jewels Series (a wide colour range, including scarlet, orange, salmon-pink, pink or white flowers).

PLANT PROFILE
HEIGHT 90cm (36in)
SPREAD 30cm (12in)
SITE Full sun
SOIL Fertile, free-draining
HARDINESS Half hardy
FLOWERING Summer

A | *Alonsoa warscewiczii* Mask flower

OCCASIONALLY WHITE FLOWERED, this small, bushy Peruvian annual is grown for two reasons. It perks up beds and borders with its dark green leaves and generous show of spurred, bright scarlet blooms, and it provides plenty of cut flowers. Often sold as a winter-flowering conservatory or houseplant, it is easily raised from seed for a summer garden display. Sow the seeds in early spring in a greenhouse for planting out after the frosts; for winter-flowering pot plants, sow the seeds in late summer. Grow outdoors in average, free-draining soil.

OTHER VARIETY *A. linearis* (brick-red flowers with black-spotted throats).

PLANT PROFILE

HEIGHT 60cm (24in)

SPREAD 30cm (12in)

SITE Full sun

SOIL Average, free-draining

HARDINESS Half hardy

FLOWERING Summer to autumn

Amaranthus caudatus Love-lies-bleeding

A

THIS FUN PLANT HAS BIZARRE FLOWERS that take the form of extremely long catkins or tassels, up to 60cm (24in) in length. Rather ghoulishly, they are said to resemble a long, frozen trickle of blood. The light green leaves are 15cm (6in) long. Love-lies-bleeding is best grown as a feature plant in containers, and can be used as a cut flower. Bring the plant under cover during winter, ready to plant out the following spring; however, it is short-lived and will soon need replacing. Sow the seeds in mid-spring in a greenhouse or indoors, and grow in moist soil, watering well in dry spells.

OTHER VARIETY 'Viridis' (tassels of vivid green flowers, fading to cream).

PLANT PROFILE

HEIGHT 1.5m (5ft)

SPREAD 75cm (30in)

SITE Full sun

SOIL Average, moist

HARDINESS Half hardy

FLOWERING Summer to early autumn

A | *Amaranthus hypochondriacus* Prince's feather

THESE EXTRAORDINARY PLANTS are grown both for their foliage and flowers. The dark purple leaves are about 15cm (6in) long, while the tiny, wine-red blooms are held in plume-like clusters which reliably keep going until autumn. If you find the related *A. caudatus* much too showy and vulgar, this is the one to go for. Sow the seeds in mid-spring under glass, and grow in moist soil which should be watered well in dry spells.

OTHER VARIETY 'Green Thumb' (brilliant yellow-green flowers).

PLANT PROFILE

HEIGHT 1.2m (4ft)

SPREAD 45cm (18in)

SITE Full sun

SOIL Average

HARDINESS Half hardy

FLOWERING Summer to early autumn

Amaranthus tricolor 'Illumination' Chinese spinach

A

JAZZILY COLOURED LEAVES are the best reason to grow this bushy amaranthus. The uppermost ones are bright red with a gold centre, and the lower ones are copper-bronze brown. All grow to about 20cm (8in) long. For maximum impact, plant 'Illumination' in a bold group rather than dotting them around in the border. Pick the insignificant flowers when they start developing or they will detract from the main show. Sow the seeds in mid-spring under glass, and for the best leaf colour grow in soil that has had plenty of organic matter incorporated. Water well during dry spells.

OTHER VARIETY 'Early Splendor' (bright crimson upper leaves and bronze lower foliage).

PLANT PROFILE	
HEIGHT 45cm (18in)	
SPREAD 45cm (18in)	
SITE Full sun	
SOIL Average	
HARDINESS Half hardy	
FLOWERING Summer to early autumn	

A

Amberboa moschata 'Imperialis' Sweet sultan

EXCELLENT FOR CUTTING, the flowers of sweet sultan (once sold as centaurea) carry a delightful fragrance that means it should ideally be grown towards the front of a border or beside a path where you can best appreciate it. Its large, fluffy flowers, bushy growth and deeply cut leaves on straight stems have established it as a cottage-garden favourite. Sow the seeds in early spring where plants are to flower, choosing your site carefully because it hates having its roots disturbed. Grow in neutral to alkaline, average, free-draining soil.

OTHER VARIETY *A. moschata* (scented, fringed flowers, in white, yellow, pink or purple).

PLANT PROFILE

HEIGHT 60cm (24in)

SPREAD 23cm (9in)

SITE Full sun

SOIL Neutral to alkaline, average, free-draining,

HARDINESS Fully hardy

FLOWERING Midsummer to early autumn

Ammobium alatum Winged everlasting

A

THIS QUIRKY, SELF-SEEDING PLANT is used more for dried-flower arrangements than garden displays. Its pale green, dandelion-like leaves are 18cm (7in) long and covered in white woolly hairs, while the 'everlasting' whitish flowers have an orange centre and keep appearing all summer. Cut the stems for drying just before the buds are fully open, and hang upside down in a cool, airy place. Sow the seeds in early spring under glass, or in mid-spring where plants are to flower in poor, light, free-draining soil.

OTHER VARIETY 'Bikini' (small, with white, yellow-centred flowers).

PLANT PROFILE
HEIGHT 90cm (36in)
SPREAD 45cm (18in)
SITE Full sun
SOIL Poor, light, free-draining
HARDINESS Half hardy
FLOWERING Summer

A | *Anagallis* 'Skylover' **Pimpernel**

TRADITIONALLY GROWN AS AN ANNUAL – because it is not totally hardy – this plant makes a branching, mat-forming spread of blue flowers with violet-pink centres. Its small size and growing requirements mean that it is best grown in a rock or gravel garden. Sow the seeds in spring in a cold frame, and grow in a greenhouse or on a windowsill for planting out the following spring. Thereafter, take cuttings of plants in summer. In the wild, the related *A. monellii* grows on Mediterranean dunes and rocky sites; 'Skylover', therefore, needs average, free-draining soil in the garden. Remember to water it in dry spells.

OTHER VARIETY 'Phillipii' (deep blue flowers).

PLANT PROFILE

HEIGHT 15cm (6in)

SPREAD 40cm (16in)

SITE Full sun

SOIL Average, free-draining

HARDINESS Frost hardy

FLOWERING Summer

Anchusa capensis 'Blue Angel' Alkanet

WITH A PROLIFIC SHOW of tiny, ultramarine-blue flowers above rough and bristly leaves, 'Blue Angel' is a bee-attracting biennial that's often grown as an annual. Its parent, *A. capensis*, is native to South Africa where it grows on rough ground and sandy sites – similar free-draining soil is essential for 'Blue Angel'. Water it in dry spells to improve the display, and cut back the dead blooms after the first flush of flowers to encourage a second one. Either sow the seeds in late summer in pots and grow them on in a greenhouse, or sow on a windowsill over winter for flowering the following summer, or sow in late winter under glass to flower several months later.

OTHER VARIETY 'Blue Bird' (indigo-blue flowers).

PLANT PROFILE
HEIGHT 20cm (8in)
SPREAD 15cm (6in)
SITE Full sun
SOIL Average, moist but free-draining
HARDINESS Frost hardy
FLOWERING Summer

Dill's mild, warm flavour is perfect for use in cooking. Strip the leaves from the stems and use them fresh or dried, or preserve them in butter, oil or vinegar.

A

Anethum graveolens Dill

THIS AIRY, ATTRACTIVE HERB with its finely divided feathery leaves will add a cottage-garden touch to a sunny border. In cooking, dill is traditionally used in fish dishes, stews and for making home-made pickled cucumbers – if you prefer a mild flavour stick to the leaves, but for a sharper taste try the seeds. Sow the seeds at three week intervals from early spring to midsummer where plants are to flower, in free-draining, fertile soil. Water well during dry spells. Unless you remove the fading flowers it will self-seed freely; take care to keep dill away from fennel or the two will cross-breed with poor results.

PLANT PROFILE

HEIGHT 60cm (24in) or more

SPREAD 30cm (12in)

SITE Full sun

SOIL Fertile, free-draining

HARDINESS Fully hardy

FLOWERING Midsummer

Anoda cristata 'Opal Cup'

A

THE DARK–VEINED, SAUCER–SHAPED FLOWERS and almost triangular leaves of 'Opal Cup' are great for adding height and colour to wildflower and cottage gardens (though farmers definitely regard it as a weed). Be sure to provide twiggy support for young plants, and keep snipping off the fading flowers to encourage more blooms. Grow plants in a very mild, protected part of the garden and they may survive the winter and reappear the following summer. Either sow the seeds in early spring under glass, or in mid-spring where the plants will flower in moist but free-draining, slightly poor soil.

OTHER VARIETY 'Silver Cup' (pure white flowers).

PLANT PROFILE

HEIGHT 1.5m (5ft)

SPREAD 60cm (24in)

SITE Full sun

SOIL Poor, moist but free-draining

HARDINESS Half hardy

FLOWERING Summer to autumn

Anthemis arabica (syn. *Cladanthus arabicus*) Palm Springs daisy

THE PALM SPRINGS DAISY deserves greater popularity – not only is it a pretty plant but it's a fascinating one, too. Look closely, and you will find that under each yellow flower is a new flowering shoot. When these go on to flower, new shoots will, in turn, develop beneath them and so on, producing a multi-stemmed effect. The flower show lasts right through the summer until the first frosts. Sow the seeds in early spring under glass, or later where they are to flower in light, free-draining soil.

OTHER VARIETY 'Criss Cross' (handsome golden flowers and deeply divided green foliage).

PLANT PROFILE
HEIGHT 60cm (24in)
SPREAD 40cm (16in)
SITE Full sun
SOIL Light, average, free-draining
HARDINESS Half hardy
FLOWERING Summer to autumn

Anthriscus cerefolium Common chervil

A

SMALL AND PRETTY WITH FERN-LIKE LEAVES, common chervil bears tiny white flowers in midsummer. The aniseed-flavoured leaves can be added sparingly to fish, potato or egg dishes (chop and add them right at the end of cooking or the flavour will be washed out). High in vitamin C, chervil is also valued for its medicinal properties. Sow the seeds in spring, where plants are to flower, in light, free-draining soil. If you keep snipping off the flowering stems, you will be guaranteed a good supply of leaves. Avoid full sun or chervil's urge to flower will be even greater.

PLANT PROFILE	
HEIGHT 50cm (20in)	
SPREAD 24cm (10in)	
SITE Sun or partial shade	
SOIL Light, free-draining	
HARDINESS Fully hardy	
FLOWERING Midsummer	

A

Antirrhinum 'Peaches & Cream' Snapdragon

A COMPACT, DWARF PLANT, 'Peaches & Cream' has soft grey–green leaves and delicate, pastel, bicoloured flowers. Sow the seeds in late summer or early autumn on a warm, sunny windowsill or in a heated greenhouse for planting out the following year after the frosts; or sow in early spring to flower that summer. Grow in fast-draining, fertile soil and keep snipping off the fading blooms to boost flower production.

OTHER VARIETY 'Bells' (purple, purple and white, red, rose-pink, pink, bronze, yellow or white flowers).

PLANT PROFILE

HEIGHT 25cm (10in)

SPREAD 20cm (8in)

SITE Full sun

SOIL Fertile, very free-draining

HARDINESS Half hardy

FLOWERING Early summer to autumn

Antirrhinum Sonnet Series Snapdragon

A BIG GROUP OF SONNET SERIES SNAPDRAGONS will create a lively show of mixed colours (bronze, pink, reds, burgundy, white, and yellow) in formal borders or cottage gardens. They are early and very free-flowering bushy plants that stand up well to damp, wet weather. Sow the seeds in late summer or early autumn under glass to plant out the following spring, or sow in early spring to flower in summer. Antirrhinums are best grown in fast-draining, fertile soil. Prolong flowering by removing fading blooms.

OTHER VARIETIES 'Miniature Magic Carpet' (shorter at 15cm, 6in); Rocket Series (taller, up to 1.2m, 4ft); Tahiti Series (dwarf, flowers are red, orange, rose-pink, and bronze, with a pink and white bicolour).

PLANT PROFILE

HEIGHT 30–60cm (12–24in)

SPREAD 30cm (12in)

SITE Full sun

SOIL Fertile, very free-draining

HARDINESS Half hardy

FLOWERING Early summer to autumn

Arctotis fastuosa var. *alba* 'Zulu Prince' Monarch of the veldt

FUN AND SHOWY, THE FLOWERS of monarch of the veldt open wide in the sun but generally close in mid-afternoon and on cloudy days (modern cultivars tend to stay open for longer). 'Zulu Prince' gives a lively display, especially in gravel or white gardens, with its whitish flowers that are backed by silver-white leaves. Alternatively, try the Harlequin Hybrids which come in a range of colours from red to pink, and white, invariably with a dark centre. Sow the seeds in autumn or early spring under glass, and grow in light, very free-draining but relatively moist soil.

OTHER VARIETY *A. fastuosa* (silvery white leaves, rich orange flowers with deep purple or black disc florets).

PLANT PROFILE

HEIGHT 60cm (24in)

SPREAD 30cm (12in)

SITE Full sun

SOIL Light, moist but very free-draining

HARDINESS Min 5°C (41°F)

FLOWERING Midsummer to early autumn

Argemone grandiflora Prickly poppy

THE TRADITIONAL POPPY IS A FAMILIAR SIGHT, but this prickly one – aptly named because of its spiny stems and leaves – may come as a surprise. It has large, papery white or yellow flowers, and white-veined, blue-green leaves. It looks spectacular in gravel gardens but is best avoided if children are playing nearby. Sow the seeds in early spring on a warm windowsill or in a greenhouse, and grow outdoors in the poorest, grittiest, stoniest soil in the garden, making sure it is light and free draining.

OTHER VARIETY *A. mexicana* 'Yellow Lustre' (yellow-orange flowers).

PLANT PROFILE
HEIGHT 1.5m (5ft)
SPREAD 40cm (16in)
SITE Full sun
SOIL Very poor, free-draining
HARDINESS Half hardy
FLOWERING Summer

A | *Argemone mexicana* Prickly poppy

THIS PRICKLY POPPY has devilishly spiny stems and leaves which means it should be kept away from the front of borders. Make sure it can be clearly seen though because it is an eye-catching plant, especially in Mediterranean-style and gravel gardens. The cupped flowers vary in yellowness and with luck you may even get an orange one. If you dare get your nose close enough, you will detect a slight scent. Sow the seeds in early spring under glass, and grow in poor, gritty, stony, free-draining soil.

OTHER VARIETY 'White Lustre' (pure white flowers).

PLANT PROFILE

HEIGHT 1m (3ft)

SPREAD 40cm (16in)

SITE Full sun

SOIL Very poor, free-draining

HARDINESS Half hardy

FLOWERING Late summer and early autumn

Argyranthemum frutescens Marguerite

A

WITH CHEERY, BRIGHT WHITE FLOWERS complete with yellow eyes and finely divided leaves, marguerites perk up pots (from the grand to the everyday) and any colour scheme. Keep snipping off the fading flowers and more will appear. A tender, shrubby plant, it can be dug up and kept in a conservatory over winter for planting out the following spring. Cuttings can easily be taken to raise more plants – take them in late summer from non-flowering shoots, and raise under glass for planting out the following summer.

OTHER VARIETIES 'Jamaica Primrose' (primrose-yellow flowerheads with darker yellow centres); 'Mary Wootton' (light pink flowerheads which fade to almost white, with pink centres).

PLANT PROFILE
HEIGHT 70cm (28in)
SPREAD 70cm (28in)
SITE Full sun
SOIL Average, free-draining
HARDINESS Half hardy
FLOWERING Summer to autumn

A | *Asperula orientalis* Woodruff

A COTTAGE-GARDEN FAVOURITE (though a weed in its native Lebanon), woodruff should go right at the front of the border where it will keep on flowering from midsummer to autumn. When grown close to a path or lawn visitors can bend down and enjoy the faint, sweet scent from the powder puff-like, tubular, bright blue (occasionally white) flowers, which are held on upright stems. Sow the seeds in early spring or autumn on a warm windowsill or in a greenhouse, and grow outdoors in free-draining, moisture-retentive soil in a sheltered site.

PLANT PROFILE

HEIGHT 30cm (12in)

SPREAD 10cm (4in)

SITE Sun or partial shade

SOIL Moist but free-draining

HARDINESS Fully hardy

FLOWERING Midsummer to autumn

Atriplex hortensis var. *rubra* Red mountain spinach

THE FAST-GROWING, BLOOD-RED to purple-red leaves are what counts with this plant – so remove the insignificant pink flowers as soon as they appear to prevent them spoiling the show. The plant makes a vibrant display in borders, especially when contrasted with white flowers and silver leaves. When picked young, the spinach-flavoured leaves – up to 18cm (7in) long – add colour to salads. Once established, atriplex self-seeds freely – regroup seedlings to form an informal hedge. Sow the seeds from spring to summer *in situ* in moist but free-draining, fertile soil. Water well during dry spells.

OTHER VARIETY Plume Series (yellow, green or burgundy-red flowers and foliage).

PLANT PROFILE
HEIGHT 1.2m (4ft)
SPREAD 30cm (12in)
SITE Full sun
SOIL Fertile, moist but free-draining
HARDINESS Half hardy
FLOWERING Summer

B *Barbarea vulgaris* 'Variegata' St. Barbara's herb

A LOVELY, SPREADING FOLIAGE PLANT, St. Barbara's herb has yellow markings on its green leaves and cross-shaped yellow flowers that appear in early spring. Although it is a hardy perennial, it is short-lived and best grown each year as a biennial to guarantee a good display. Typically grown right at the front of a border, sow the seeds in late summer where plants are to flower the following year, and grow in moist but free-draining, preferably slightly acid soil.

PLANT PROFILE

HEIGHT 45cm (18in)

SPREAD 20cm (8in)

SITE Full sun or partial shade

SOIL Slightly acid, moist but free-draining

HARDINESS Fully hardy

FLOWERING Early spring to early summer

Bassia scoparia f. *trichophylla* Burning bush

B

RESEMBLING A GIANT, FUZZY, UPRIGHT CONE, this extremely useful annual adds instant height in the summer, creating low hedges or screens that can measure between 30cm–1.5m (1–5ft) tall. The inconspicuous flowers are just an aside – the big attraction is the mass of thin emerald-green leaves that turn bright red or purple at the start of autumn. Sow the seeds in early spring on a warm windowsill or in a greenhouse, or at the end of spring where they are to grow in fertile, free-draining soil in a sunny, sheltered position.

PLANT PROFILE

HEIGHT 1.5m (5ft)

SPREAD 45cm (18in)

SITE Full sun

SOIL Fertile, free-draining

HARDINESS Half hardy

FLOWERING Late summer or autumn

Begonia Cocktail Series

GROWN FOR THEIR ROUNDED BRONZE LEAVES and single, bicoloured, weather-resistant flowers, begonias are typically used to create patterns at the front of beds and to jazz up hanging baskets and windowboxes. Cocktail Series produces pink, red, and white flowers from summer until the autumn frosts. As a semperflorens begonia, it flowers particularly well in partial shade, although it also tolerates direct overhead sunlight. Sow the seeds in early spring under glass, and plant out in fertile, free-draining, neutral to acid soil. Apply a nitrogen-rich feed when young plants are developing.

OTHER VARIETIES 'Olympia White' (compact, with single white flowers); 'Organdy' (single white, pink, rose-pink, and scarlet flowers).

PLANT PROFILE
HEIGHT 30cm (12in)
SPREAD 30cm (12in)
SITE Light dappled shade
SOIL Neutral to acid, fertile, free-draining
HARDINESS Min 13°C (55°F)
FLOWERING Summer to autumn

Begonia Illumination Series

B

THE HABIT OF THESE TRAILING PLANTS is very different to that of the perennial begonia with it red-bronze winter leaves, which is a mainstay of formal planting schemes. The Illumination Series is best grown in hanging baskets, raised beds or in tall, thin Victorian chimney pots dotted around the garden. Grown in such elevated containers, the 8cm (3in) wide flowers will tumble prettily over the sides – although when they are planted at lower levels they also look good trailing across the ground. Sow the seeds in early spring under glass, and grow outdoors in fertile, free-draining, neutral to slightly acid soil, avoiding direct sun.

OTHER VARIETY 'Illumination Orange' (vivid orange flowers).

PLANT PROFILE
HEIGHT 60cm (24in)
SPREAD 30cm (12in)
SITE Light dappled shade
SOIL Neutral to slightly acid, fertile, free-draining
HARDINESS Min 10°C (50°F)
FLOWERING Summer

Begonia Non Stop Series

THESE REMARKABLY COMPACT PLANTS live up to their name, and flower right through summer until the first frosts. They have large, double flowers, 8cm (3in) wide, and are perfect for the front of a border. Sow the seeds in early spring under glass, and plant out in fertile, free-draining, neutral to acid soil. Dig up the tubers (bulb-like structures which are food storage organs) in autumn, and keep dry over winter in a cool, frost-free place. Replant (hollow side up) in pots the following spring, and gradually increase their water supply. Plant out in early summer.

OTHER VARIETIES 'Flamboyant' (single, dark scarlet flowers); 'Pin-up' (single white flowers).

PLANT PROFILE

HEIGHT 30cm (12in)

SPREAD 30cm (12in)

SITE Light dappled shade

SOIL Neutral to acid, fertile, free-draining

HARDINESS Min 10°C (50°F)

FLOWERING Summer

Bellis perennis 'Goliath' Common daisy

B

THE COMMON DAISY may not be welcome in crisp, neat, bowling green–type lawns, but the ornamental daisy is a bonus in rock gardens, gaps in patio paving, containers, and for edging. 'Goliath' has large, showy, pompon–like flowers and bright green leaves. Sow the seeds in spring or early summer in pots, and plant out in late summer or early autumn to flower from late winter. Grow in free-draining, average soil, and water well in dry spells.

OTHER VARIETY Pomponette Series (double, pink, white or red flowers).

PLANT PROFILE
HEIGHT 20cm (8in)
SPREAD 20cm (8in)
SITE Full sun or partial shade
SOIL Average, free-draining
HARDINESS Fully hardy
FLOWERING Late winter to summer

B

Bellis perennis Tasso Series **Common daisy**

THE RED, PINK, AND WHITE double flowers of the Tasso Series are very distinctive. In fact, with their 6cm (2½in) wide pompons they look more like miniature dahlias than simple daisies. Sow the seeds in spring or early summer in pots, and plant outdoors in late summer or early autumn, ready to flower from late winter and throughout spring. For best results, grow in free-draining, average soil, and water well during dry spells.

OTHER VARIETY 'Tasso Strawberries & Cream' (red, and white flowers).

PLANT PROFILE
HEIGHT 20cm (8in)
SPREAD 20cm (8in)
SITE Full sun or partial shade
SOIL Average, free-draining
HARDINESS Fully hardy
FLOWERING Late winter to summer

Beta vulgaris subsp. *cicla* Swiss chard

B

WITH ITS GLOSSY GREEN LEAVES and fantastic red ribs, Swiss chard is too good to tuck away in the kitchen garden, and it is attractive enough for containers and ornamental borders. An edible member of the beetroot family, its swollen leaf stalks and green leaves are delicious cooked. The cultivars, which have all-red foliage, are even more flamboyant than the parent. Sow the seeds *in situ* in early spring for summer and winter cropping, or sow in late summer for harvesting over winter into summer (yields will be lower). Grow in well-watered, light, free-draining, nitrogen-rich soil.

OTHER VARIETIES 'Bull's Blood' (dark red foliage); 'MacGregor's Favourite' (brilliant blood-red foliage); 'Vulcan' (brilliant red foliage).

PLANT PROFILE	
HEIGHT 23cm (9in)	
SPREAD 45cm (18in)	
SITE Full sun or partial shade	
SOIL Fertile, light, moist	
HARDINESS Fully hardy	
FOLIAGE All year	

B | *Bidens ferulifolia* 'Golden Goddess'

A BIG HIT WITH HANGING BASKET and windowbox fans, 'Golden Goddess' has long, thin, wiry stems that angle all over the place. These stems are topped by small, bright yellow flowers measuring 5cm (2in) across. An attractive, light, airy plant, it is particularly effective when the stems snake through adjacent plants to create a lively, colourful mix. Sow the seeds in spring on a warm windowsill or in a greenhouse, and grow in any decent, moist but free-draining soil that is well-watered in dry spells.

OTHER VARIETY *B. ferulifolia* (daisy-like, golden-yellow flowers).

PLANT PROFILE

HEIGHT 30cm (12in)

SPREAD Indefinite

SITE Full sun

SOIL Average, moist but free-draining

HARDINESS Frost hardy

FLOWERING Midsummer to autumn

Borago officinalis Borage

A FAVOURITE BEE PLANT, borage is a herb with tasty, cucumber-flavoured leaves that are used in salads, yogurt dishes and refreshing drinks (you can even make tea with it). Pick the fading flowers later in the season (they keep appearing right up until the frosts) or they will self-seed prolifically, and next year you will have borage sprouting everywhere. Sow the seeds in late spring where they are to flower, or sow in early spring under glass – germination is fast, usually giving plants in six weeks. Borage is unfussy and will grow well in any decent, even fairly dry, soil.

PLANT PROFILE
HEIGHT 60cm (24in)
SPREAD 45cm (18in)
SITE Full sun or partial shade
SOIL Almost any
HARDINESS Fully hardy
FLOWERING Summer to autumn

B

Brachyscome iberidifolia Swan river daisy

THE SWAN RIVER DAISY provides a gentle summery display with masses of very faintly scented, small, daisy-like flowers with yellow eyes. The flowers are nicely offset by the lacy, feathery, grey-green leaves which are 10cm (4in) long. It can be grown just about anywhere in the garden, from pots and hanging baskets to cracks in paving, rock gardens, and right at the front of a border. Keep pinching out the tips of young plants to make them bushier and more flowery. Sow the seeds in spring under glass, and plant out in fertile, free-draining soil where there is shelter from strong winds.

OTHER VARIETY Splendour Series (black-eyed, white, lilac-pink or purple flowers).

PLANT PROFILE	
HEIGHT 45cm (18in)	
SPREAD 35cm (14in)	
SITE Full sun	
SOIL Fertile, free-draining	
HARDINESS Half hardy	
FLOWERING Summer	

Bracteantha bracteata 'Dargan Hill Monarch' Golden everlasting

B

GOLDEN EVERLASTING IS A FITTING NAME for this delightful plant. The flowers – each with a yellow eye encircled by golden-yellow petals – put on a bright, sunny show all through summer against a backdrop of finely cut, grey-green leaves. Although it is a perennial, it is relatively short-lived and will need replacing with fresh stock grown from seed every few years. Sow the seeds in spring on a warm windowsill or in a greenhouse, and plant out in moist but free-draining, average soil. The flowers are good for cutting and drying.

OTHER VARIETY 'Sky Net' (pink-flushed, creamy-white flowers).

PLANT PROFILE
HEIGHT 1.5m (5ft)
SPREAD 30cm (12in)
SITE Full sun
SOIL Average, moist but free-draining
HARDINESS Half hardy
FLOWERING Late spring to autumn

B

Bracteantha bracteata Monstrosum Series Golden everlasting

USE THIS VERSATILE ANNUAL to create meandering drifts, fill gaps in borders or, because of its long flowering season, encircle ornamental features such as statues. The stems stand smartly erect and are topped by daisy-like flowers. Other cultivars provide extra tones and height – the flame red, pink, orange, yellow, or white Tetraploid Double Series is a vigorous 1.5m (5ft) high. Sow the seeds in spring under glass, and plant out in average soil and water it well. It makes an exceptional dried flower for winter arrangements.

OTHER VARIETIES Bright Bikinis Series (double, red, pink, orange, yellow or white flowers); King Size Series (double flowers in yellow, pink, orange, red or silvery-white); 'Silvery Rose' (double, silvery-pink flowers).

PLANT PROFILE
HEIGHT 90cm (36in)
SPREAD 30cm (12in)
SITE Full sun
SOIL Average, moist but free-draining
HARDINESS Half hardy
FLOWERING Late spring to autumn

Brassica oleracea cultivars Ornamental cabbage and kale

B

OUTRAGEOUS AND HIDEOUSLY VULGAR or just plain good fun, these cabbages are grown for their brightly coloured leaves and not for the pot – the flavour is much too bitter and the colours turn a wishy-washy grey when cooked. The foliage shades will intensify when the temperatures start to dip in autumn. Sow the seeds in late spring for nice tight heads, and grow in fertile, free-draining, preferably lime-rich soil.

OTHER VARIETIES Osaka Series (fast-growing, with wavy, blue-green outer leaves and compact, white, pink or red centres); 'Tokyo' (rounded, blue-green outer leaves and soft, pink, red or white centres).

PLANT PROFILE
HEIGHT 45cm (18in)
SPREAD 45cm (18in)
SITE Full sun
SOIL Lime-rich, fertile, free-draining
HARDINESS Fully hardy
FLOWERING Summer

B

Briza maxima Greater quaking grass

AN ATTRACTIVE ORNAMENTAL GRASS, *B. maxima* is grown for its delicate heart-shaped seedheads which are red or purple when first open, and a rich straw colour when dry. The grass rustles and trembles in the slightest breeze (hence its common name) and when planted in blocks in a sunny border it adds the unexpected element of movement. Sow the seeds in autumn where the plants are to grow in free-draining soil. Once established it is a reliable self-seeder. It is also a good subject for cutting and drying.

OTHER VARIETY *Briza media* (shorter annual grass)

PLANT PROFILE

HEIGHT 60cm (24in)

SPREAD 25cm (10in)

SITE Full sun

SOIL Free-draining

HARDINESS Fully hardy

FLOWERING Late spring to late summer

Briza minor Lesser quaking grass

B

A LOVELY, SMALLISH ANNUAL GRASS, this is ideal for growing around the base of fruit trees, in wild gardens, or in borders where it adds an attractive scattering of tiny seedheads. The stems can also be used in dried flower arrangements. Initially pale green, frequently with a purple tint, the seedheads gradually turn beige in autumn. Sow the seeds *in situ* in autumn or spring in free–draining soil. Once established it will self-seed freely.

PLANT PROFILE	
HEIGHT T45cm (18in)	
SPREAD 25cm (10in)	
SITE Full sun	
SOIL Free-draining	
HARDINESS Fully hardy	
FLOWERING Early summer to early autumn	

B | *Bromus lanceolatus* (syn. *B. macrostachys*) Brome grass

THE CLUSTERED, PURPLE-TINGED SPIKELETS of brome grass look best in a wild flower garden or meadow in a mixed planting with *Panicum capillare* (witch grass) and *Briza maxima* (greater quaking grass). Brome grass is also worth growing for its dried flowerheads – remove them before they have peaked and hang them up to dry. Sow the seeds in spring where plants are to flower. Originally from dry wasteland areas in the Mediterranean, it needs similar light, free-draining soil conditions in the garden.

PLANT PROFILE	
HEIGHT 50cm (20in)	
SPREAD 10cm (4in)	
SITE Sun	
SOIL Free-draining	
HARDINESS Fully hardy	
FLOWERING Summer	

Browallia speciosa 'White Troll' Sapphire flower

B

THE SAPPHIRE FLOWER IS A PERENNIAL in its native South America, but when grown in north-west Europe it is usually treated as an annual. Sprawling, bushy and free flowering, its subtle charms are best appreciated in a hanging basket or when used as an edging plant. If grown in a container it can be brought indoors to overwinter, ready for flowering again the following summer. Do not overfeed or the plant will produce plenty of leaves but no flowers. Sow the seeds in early spring under glass and plant out in rich, free-draining soil. Water well during dry spells.

OTHER VARIETIES 'Blue Troll' (clear blue flowers); 'Vanja' (deep blue flowers).

PLANT PROFILE
HEIGHT 60cm (24in)
SPREAD 25cm (10in)
SITE Full sun or partial shade
SOIL Fertile, free-draining
HARDINESS Min 13–16°C (55–61°F)
FLOWERING Summer

B | *Bupleurum rotundifolium* Thorow-wax

YOU ARE MORE LIKELY to find this plant in a seed catalogue, particularly a specialist one, than the latest fashionable gardening books. *B. rotundifolium* makes a bushy-stemmed plant for the border with very small, star-shaped flowers. The new leaves carry a faint pink tinge before turning slightly blue. 'Green Gold' is very similar in habit but has yellow flowers. Sow the seeds in spring in pots in a cold frame, and plant out in average, free-draining soil.

PLANT PROFILE

HEIGHT 60cm (24in)

SPREAD 30cm (12in)

SITE Full sun

SOIL Average, free-draining

HARDINESS Frost hardy

FLOWERING Summer

Calandrinia grandiflora

FROM THE DRY, ROCKY SLOPES OF CHILE comes this clump-forming annual with five- to seven-petalled flowers and fleshy stems. Its bright green leaves are elliptical in shape and measure up to 20cm (8in) in length. Sow the seeds in early spring under glass, and grow outdoors in fertile, fast-draining, slightly acid soil. It does well on dry, sunny banks and can also be grown as a houseplant. Beware of slugs and snails getting too close to the new, young growth because they will quickly demolish it.

OTHER VARIETY *C. ciliata* (purple, red, pink or white flowers).

PLANT PROFILE
HEIGHT 1m (3ft)
SPREAD 45cm (18in)
SITE Full sun
SOIL Slightly acid, fertile, very free-draining
HARDINESS Min 6°C (43°F)
FLOWERING Summer

C   *Calandrinia umbellata* Rock purslane

THIS SHORT-GROWING SOUTH-AMERICAN PERENNIAL needs to be grown as an annual because it hates the cold and having its roots locked in wet soil over winter. Its large crimson-magenta flowers – which close up when it gets cloudy – last only 48 hours before being replaced by new blooms. In autumn, dig up plants and transfer to pots for overwintering in a conservatory, and plant out again in early summer. Sow the seed in early spring under glass, or sow in autumn for flowers the following summer. Plant somewhere hot and sunny in fertile, slightly acid soil with excellent drainage.

OTHER VARIETY 'Amaranth' (rich crimson-magenta flowers).

PLANT PROFILE
HEIGHT 20cm (8in)
SPREAD 20cm (8in)
SITE Full sun
SOIL Slightly acid, free-draining
HARDINESS Frost hardy
FLOWERING Summer

Calceolaria integrifolia Pouch flower

C

QUIRKY, FLAMBOYANT AND UNUSUAL, this plant is a perennial in its native Mexico but in north-west Europe it has to be grown as an annual. The small, bright yellow flowers resemble tiny balls from a distance and number up to 35 in each cluster. This plant is the parent of some lovely shorter-growing cultivars, including the midsummer-flowering 'Sunshine' which, at 30cm (12in), will brighten hanging baskets and pots, and the 40cm (16in) tall 'Goldcut' which is good for cutting. Sow the seeds in spring or autumn under glass, and plant out in light, average, acid soil in a cool position.

OTHER VARIETIES 'Golden Bunch' (compact with pale golden-yellow flowers); 'Midas' (deep yellow flowers, good for hanging baskets).

PLANT PROFILE
HEIGHT 1.2m (4ft)
SPREAD 30cm (9–12in)
SITE Sun or partial shade
SOIL Acid, average
HARDINESS Half hardy
FLOWERING Summer

C

Calendula officinalis 'Art Shades' English marigold

MARIGOLDS ARE THE ULTIMATE easy-care, quick-growing annuals. Use them as star ingredients and fillers in any style of garden, from cottage to formal. 'Art Shades' are taller than most, with large, frilly flowers. Pinch them out when they're young to make them bushier, and keep deadheading all summer. Do not overcrowd them or they will end up getting mildew. Sow the seeds in spring where they are to flower – they will then keep self-seeding year after year. Grow all marigolds in free-draining, average soil.

OTHER VARIETIES Kablouna Series (tall with double orange, gold or yellow flowers); Pacific Beauty Series (double flowers in an unusual colour range, including bicolours).

PLANT PROFILE

HEIGHT 60cm (24in)

SPREAD 60cm (24in)

SITE Sun or partial shade

SOIL Average, free-draining

HARDINESS Fully hardy

FLOWERING Summer to autumn

Callistephus chinensis 'Compliment Light Blue' China aster

AS WITH ALL CULTIVARS of *C. CHINENSIS*, 'Compliment Light Blue' is a big favourite with cut-flower lovers. Typically fast-growing and bushy, the flowers of this particular cultivar are what is known as quill-petalled, with a tangled mesh of thin petals. Sow the seeds in early spring under glass, or sow *in situ* in late spring in fertile, moist but free-draining soil that tends towards alkaline. Choose a warm, sheltered site.

OTHER VARIETIES Comet Series (dwarf, double flowers in a range of colours, good for containers); Duchesse Series (incurved flowers in colours ranging from yellow to red and purple, good for cut flowers); Pompon Series (button-like flowers in a wide range of colours).

PLANT PROFILE
HEIGHT 70cm (28in)
SPREAD 20cm (8in)
SITE Full sun
SOIL Neutral to alkaline, fertile, moist but free-draining
HARDINESS Half hardy
FLOWERING Summer and early autumn

C | *Callistephus chinensis* Ostrich Plume Series China aster

CHINA ASTERS PROVIDE SOFT AUTUMN COLOURS and basketfuls of cut flowers, though in the garden they often go down with a disease called wilt. The good news about the Ostrich Plume Series is that it fights off wilt better than most; growing them in different beds each year also helps avoid the problem. They are additionally blessed with long feathery petals and wide-branching growth that makes them good for cutting. Deadhead regularly to keep the flowers coming. Sow the seeds in early spring under glass, or in late spring where they are to flower in fertile, free-draining soil mixed with leafmould.

OTHER VARIETY Pommax Series (vigorous, tall and compact, double flowerheads in a wide colour range).

PLANT PROFILE

HEIGHT 60cm (24in)

SPREAD 30cm (12in)

SITE Full sun

SOIL Neutral to alkaline, fertile, moist but free-draining

HARDINESS Half hardy

FLOWERING Late summer to autumn

Calomeria amaranthoides Incense plant

A FAVOURITE WITH THE VICTORIANS, the incense plant is starting to make a comeback. It is a perennial from south Australia, Madagascar and Africa but in north-west Europe is best grown as a biennial. It is a large, imposing plant with drooping branches and clusters of tiny, dangling, brownish-pink to red flowers which are good for drying. Sow the seeds in autumn in pots – don't cover them over with soil – on a warm windowsill or in a greenhouse. Be patient because there is a long germination period of about eight months. In summer, plant outdoors in borders in fertile, free-draining soil. To encourage the plant to release its fragrance, spray the foliage with a fine mist of water. Avoid handling the leaves because they can cause skin irritation.

PLANT PROFILE

HEIGHT 2m (6ft)

SPREAD 1m (3ft)

SITE Full sun

SOIL Fertile, free-draining

HARDINESS Min 4°C (39°F)

FLOWERING Summer

C

C

Campanula isophylla 'Stella Blue' Falling stars

IT'S THE SMALL, STAR–SHAPED FLOWERS that give this compact plant its common name. Ideal for hanging baskets or windowboxes, the neat flowers fall over the sides, giving a long flowering show. Sow the seeds in autumn or in late winter in a greenhouse or on a windowsill, and plant out in free-draining, fertile soil. Plants can be kept over winter in a conservatory, but if left in the garden they will be killed by the cold.

OTHER VARIETY 'Stella White' (star-shaped, white flowers).

PLANT PROFILE

HEIGHT 20cm (8in)

SPREAD 30cm (12in)

SITE Sun or partial shade

SOIL Fertile, free-draining

HARDINESS Half hardy

FLOWERING Summer

Campanula medium 'Calycanthema' Canterbury bells

WITH CHUNKY, CURVACEOUS BELLS on the top two-thirds of its stems, *C. medium* is a traditional cottage-garden plant and makes a strong show in borders or large containers. 'Calycanthema' goes one better, often having double flowers, one inside the other, in white, pink or blue. Either sow the seeds in midsummer or autumn in a cold frame, planting them out in spring where they are to flower; or sow in late winter under glass, and plant out the following spring to flower in summer. Grow in fertile, moist but free-draining soil with the roots in the shade of adjacent plants and the flowers in sun.

OTHER VARIETY 'Bells of Holland' (dwarf, bearing single flowers in a variety of colours).

PLANT PROFILE
HEIGHT 75cm (30in)
SPREAD 30cm (12in)
SITE Sun or partial shade
SOIL Neutral to alkaline, fertile, moist but free-draining
HARDINESS Fully hardy
FLOWERING Spring to summer

C | *Campanula pyramidalis* Chimney bellflower

GROWN AS A PERENNIAL THIS PLANT will quickly deteriorate, which means the biennial forms are the best buy. They provide erect stems with 4cm (1½in) wide, cup-shaped, faintly scented flowers, and fill gaps to the back of a border. The name *pyramidalis* refers to the fact that there are many more flowers down at the base of the stems than high at the top, creating a loose, pyramid-like shape. For this reason you need to place plants to the front of a border, so that the whole plant can be seen. Sow the seeds in spring in a cold frame, and plant out in fertile, moist but free-draining, neutral to alkaline soil. Flower colour is best preserved in light shade.

OTHER VARIETY *C. pyramidalis alba* (pure white flowers).

PLANT PROFILE

HEIGHT 3m (10ft)

SPREAD 60cm (24in)

SITE Sun or partial shade

SOIL Neutral to alkaline, fertile, moist but free-draining

HARDINESS Frost hardy

FLOWERING Late spring to summer

Capsicum annuum ornamental cultivars Chilli pepper

ANNUAL PEPPERS ARE EASY TO GROW in 20cm (8in) pots or growing bags. There are basically two kinds: the fleshy bell-shaped peppers for salads or stews; and the smaller, often brightly coloured, finger-shaped, hotter (often explosively hot) peppers for oriental cooking. Bell-shaped peppers come in all kinds of weird shapes and sizes. Typical supermarket peppers are green, orange, or red but home-grown varieties come in a wide range of colours including purple, brown, and flaming orange-red. The seeds, sown in late winter, can take three weeks to germinate (hot peppers take the longest) and the plants need a sunny sheltered site for the fruit to ripen.

OTHER VARIETY 'Black Prince' (purple foliage and fruit).

PLANT PROFILE

HEIGHT 75cm (30in)

SPREAD 30cm (12in)

SITE Full sun

SOIL Fertile, enriched with garden compost or manure, free-draining

HARDINESS Min 4°C (39°F)

FLOWERING Summer

C *Cardiospermum halicacabum* Balloon vine

THIS CLIMBER, FOUND CLOSE TO THE TROPICS, is grown for its puffed-up, balloon-like seed pods or capsules which appear in autumn, and not for its insignificant green-white summer flowers. These capsules, which are initially light green but gradually turn cream-beige, are surprisingly tough and hard to break open. They have given rise to a number of delightful common names, including heart pea, love-in-a-puff and winter cherry. Sow the seeds in spring on a warm windowsill or in a greenhouse, and grow outdoors in fertile, moist but free-draining soil. Its tendrils will help it clamber up a trellis, pergola or tree stump.

PLANT PROFILE

HEIGHT 4m (12ft)

SITE Full sun

SOIL Fertile, moist but free-draining

HARDINESS Min 7–10°C (45–50°F)

FLOWERING Summer to autumn

Carlina acaulis Stemless Carline thistle

C

A SUPERB PLANT FOR DRY OR GRAVEL GARDENS, *C. acaulis* forms a rosette of prickly leaves up to 30cm (12in) long. The stemless daisy-like flowers, which appear in the centre of the leaves, look blue on opening but turn silver-cream and may be flushed with pink. They are made up of thin bracts surrounding a buff-brown central disc. When dried, flower arrangers can't get enough of them. Sow the seeds in autumn in a cold frame or where they are to flower. In the wild, *C. acaulis* grows in poor, stony soil, often just a thin layer above chalk, and in the garden it needs similar conditions. Plants are short-lived, often dying after flowering.

PLANT PROFILE

HEIGHT 10cm (4in)

SPREAD 25cm (10in)

SITE Full sun

SOIL Poor, free-draining

HARDINESS Fully hardy

FLOWERING Mid- and late summer

C *Carpanthea pomeridiana* 'Golden Carpet'

A SHORT, MULTIPURPOSE, DAISY-LIKE PLANT from South Africa, 'Golden Carpet' is perfect for Mediterranean-type gardens, rockeries, containers and gaps in patio paving. The bright yellow flowers with their frilly petals and cream-yellow eyes make a prolific show. The only problem is that they only open when it is sunny and shut tight the moment it is overcast. Sow the seeds in late winter under glass, and plant outdoors in average, free-draining soil (they like to be kept on the dry side, so don't overwater them).

OTHER VARIETY *C. pomeridiana* (multiple petals, yellow, daisy-like flowers).

PLANT PROFILE

HEIGHT 15cm (6in)

SPREAD 23cm (9in)

SITE Sun

SOIL Average, dry or free-draining

HARDINESS Fully hardy

FLOWERING Summer

Carthamus tinctorius 'Goldtuft' Safflower

C

ALSO KNOWN AS FALSE SAFFRON because the flowers were once used to make yellow dye, 'Goldtuft' looks better in cottage rather than formal gardens, and is often grown for its long-lasting cut flowers. The blooms are 4cm (1½in) wide and resemble thistles or fluffy pompons – some experts have described the petals as looking like the soaking wet hair of a dog after it has leapt out of the sea and had a shake. Sow the seeds in spring under glass, and plant out in light, free-draining soil.

OTHER VARIETIES 'Lasting White' (white flowers); 'Orange Ball' (orange flowers).

PLANT PROFILE	
HEIGHT	60cm (24in)
SPREAD	30cm (12in)
SITE	Full sun
SOIL	Light, free-draining
HARDINESS	Fully hardy
FLOWERING	Summer

TASTY SEEDS

Caraway seeds have a strong, distinctive flavour and are best mixed with other strongly flavoured ingredients, such as onion, or used sparingly.

C

Carum carvi Caraway

CARAWAY IS A SPINDLY, UPRIGHT PLANT that is grown for its ribbed, brown seeds which follow on from the open heads of tiny, white flowers. The seeds are the most important part of the plant and can be used in a surprising range of recipes while the feathery, aromatic, bright green leaves can be shredded and used in salads. Its root can also be cooked and eaten as a vegetable. Sow the seeds in autumn (to flower and produce seed the following summer) or spring where plants are to flower in average, free-draining soil.

PLANT PROFILE

HEIGHT 60cm (24in)

SPREAD 30cm (12in)

SITE Full sun

SOIL Average, free-draining

HARDINESS Fully hardy

FLOWERING Midsummer

Catharanthus roseus 'Parasol' Madagascar periwinkle

C

NEW, BUSHY CULTIVARS keep coming on the market in a wide mix of colours and all are very good. Shorter types can be grown as evergreen house plants but 'Parasol', with its white flowers and contrasting pink-red eyes, is one of the tallest and best suited to the border. Sow the seeds in early spring under glass and grow in dry, light, very free-draining soil on a south-facing bank, or in a Mediterranean-style garden where there is wall-to-wall sun. As excess moisture will kill the Madagascar periwinkle, it won't make a happy bedfellow with plants that need plenty of water.

OTHER VARIETY Cooler Series (compact and branching with deep rose-pink and white flowers with broad, overlapping petals).

PLANT PROFILE

HEIGHT 45cm (18in)

SPREAD 45cm (18in)

SITE Full sun

SOIL Average, very free-draining

HARDINESS Min 5–7°C (41–45°F)

FLOWERING Spring to summer

C | *Celosia argentea* 'Fairy Fountains' (Plumosa Group) Cockscomb

THERE ARE TWO MAIN KINDS of annual celosias: the cultivars of *C. argentea* var. *cristata* Plumosa Group, with their feathery plumes; and those of *C. argentea* var. *cristata*, which have much tighter flowerheads and are typically sold as pot plants. 'Fairy Fountains', which is traditionally used in massed displays, belongs to the first group and comes in a mix of colours, including pink, salmon-pink, and creamy-yellow. Sow the seeds in spring under glass, and grow outdoors in a sheltered site in fertile, moist but free-draining soil.

OTHER VARIETIES 'Apricot Brandy' (deep orange flowers); Century Series (vivid red, rose-pink or yellow flowers).

PLANT PROFILE
HEIGHT 40cm (16in)
SPREAD 30cm (12in)
SITE Full sun
SOIL Fertile, moist but free-draining
HARDINESS Half hardy
FLOWERING Summer

Celosia argentea var. *cristata* cultivars Cockscomb

C

THESE INCREDIBLY STRIKING and wonderfully bizarre flowers stand smartly erect like the combs of a rooster. They look engineered by horticultural boffins but are quite natural. Adding a wonderful or screamingly vulgar touch to the garden, they invariably look best grown in a bold group as a fun feature. Good cultivars include the 30cm (12in) high mix called 'Coral Garden', and the even shorter 'Jewel Box'. Sow the seeds in spring under glass, and plant out in a sheltered site in fertile, moist but free-draining soil.

OTHER VARIETY Olympia Series (dwarf, flowers in colours including golden-yellow, scarlet, light red, deep cerise, and purple).

PLANT PROFILE
HEIGHT 10cm–1.2m (4in–4ft)
SPREAD 15–50cm (6–20in)
SITE Full sun
SOIL Fertile, moist but free-draining
HARDINESS Half hardy
FLOWERING Summer

C

Centaurea americana 'Aloha' Knapweed

THIS IS AN IMPRESSIVE BEAUTY with stout stems and 15cm (6in) wide flowers, each with a ring of whiskery petals. When cut, the blooms will last for a week in a vase. The parent plant, *C. americana*, has slightly darker flowers which are more pink-purple. Sow the seeds *in situ* in spring in moist but free-draining soil; it is important that the plants are not subsequently moved because they hate root disturbance. Knapweed is suited to the informality of a wild flower or cottage garden, and if you have space for a bed exclusively for cut flowers, include it.

OTHER VARIETY 'Aloha Blanca' (white flowers).

PLANT PROFILE

HEIGHT 1.2m (4ft)

SPREAD 60cm (24in)

SITE Full sun or partial shade

SOIL Moist but free-draining

HARDINESS Fully hardy

FLOWERING Summer

Centaurea cyanus Standard Tall Group Cornflower

C

NOW A POPULAR WILD FLOWER GARDEN PLANT, the bright blue cornflower was once a common cornfield weed until it was sprayed to death. Most new cultivars offer a wider range of colours on bushier, shorter plants, however, one taller cultivar, the Standard Tall Group, reaches a staggering 1–1.2m (3–4ft). Its flowers come in white and shades of pink, blue, mauve, and maroon, all of which make excellent cut flowers. Sow the seeds in spring where plants are to grow, or sow in autumn for flowers at the end of the spring. The soil must be well drained.

OTHER VARIETY Florence Series (cherry-red, pink or white flowers).

PLANT PROFILE

HEIGHT 1–1.2m (3–4ft)

SPREAD 25cm (10in)

SITE Full sun or partial shade

SOIL Free-draining

HARDINESS Fully hardy

FLOWERING Late spring to midsummer

C *Centradenia inaequilateralis* 'Cascade'

ADD AN EXTRA HUE TO PASTEL SCHEMES with the pink to mauve flowers of 'Cascade'. These are backed by copper-tinged foliage which is more obvious in shady conditions – it becomes greener in full sun. If you pinch out the growing stems early in the season, it will give a full, bushy display over summer. Potted up and brought indoors in autumn it makes a good conservatory plant; however, to ensure flowers the following year 'Cascade' needs a cool winter period. Propagate from summer cuttings, and grow in fertile, moist but free-draining soil.

PLANT PROFILE

HEIGHT 38cm (15in)

SPREAD 30cm (12in)

SITE Partial shade

SOIL Fertile, moist but free-draining

HARDINESS Min 5°C (41°F)

FLOWERING Summer

Cerinthe major 'Purpurascens' Blue honeywort

C

BLUE HONEYWORT IS AN EYE-CATCHING PLANT with quirky, purple growths on the tips of its stems – which practically obscure the tiny, bee-attracting flowers – and rich blue-green foliage on lax, floppy branching stems. The plant keeps performing steadily right through summer up until the first frost, and once established in the garden there's no going back as it is a prolific self-seeder. Grow it at the front of a border where everyone can enjoy its unusual looks. Sow the seeds in early spring under glass, or sow in late spring *in situ* preferably in free-draining soil, although it will also tolerate clay.

OTHER VARIETY 'Yellow Gem' (yellow flowers).

PLANT PROFILE

HEIGHT 60cm (24in)

SPREAD Indefinite

SITE Full sun to partial shade

SOIL Fertile, moist but free-draining

HARDINESS Fully hardy

FLOWERING Summer to autumn

C *Chrysanthemum carinatum* Painted daisy

ERECT, BUSHY AND QUICK GROWING, *C. carinatum* has round, white, daisy-like flowers, 10cm (4in) wide, with a yellow inner ring and a purple centre (hence the common name). It has bright green almost succulent-like leaves. Grow this free-flowering plant as a colourful gap-filler in the border, and enjoy its easy-going charms in cottage and wild flower gardens. There are several cultivars, all of which are excellent for cutting. Sow the seeds *in situ* in spring, or earlier in a cold frame, and grow in free-draining, average soil.

OTHER VARIETY 'Polar Star' (pale yellow flowers, zoned in orange).

PLANT PROFILE
HEIGHT 60cm (24in)
SPREAD 30cm (12in)
SITE Full sun
SOIL Average, free-draining
HARDINESS Half hardy
FLOWERING Summer to early autumn

Chrysanthemum coronarium Crown daisy

C

SOMETIMES CALLED THE CROWN DAISY, this chrysanthemum produces
5cm (2in) wide, butter-yellow flowers in spring. Like *C. carinatum*
it is erect, bushy and free-flowering but its light green leaves are
fern-like. If you live in a relatively mild area, sow the seeds in
autumn in a cold frame or where plants are to flower in mid-spring.
In colder regions, sow in spring for summer flowers. Average, free-
draining soil is fine, but if it is too fertile the stems can become
floppy and will need staking.

OTHER VARIETY 'Primrose Gem' (pale yellow with a golden eye).

PLANT PROFILE	
HEIGHT	80cm (32in)
SPREAD	40cm (16in)
SITE	Full sun
SOIL	Average, free-draining
HARDINESS	Fully hardy
FLOWERING	Spring to summer

C   *Chrysanthemum multicaule* 'Moonlight'

UNLIKE THE LARGER CHRYSANTHEMUMS, some of which may grow
to 1.2m (4ft) high, 'Moonlight' is a compact, low-growing plant. With
its clear, pale yellow petals surrounding a yellow button eye, it is a
pretty choice for troughs, pots and windowboxes, and is well suited
to growing in gaps in a patio terrace. Easy to grow, sow the seeds
in early spring on a warm windowsill or in a greenhouse, or sow
in late spring where plants are to flower. It will grow well in average,
well-drained soil.

OTHER VARIETY   'Sunlight' (yellow flowers).

PLANT PROFILE
HEIGHT 10cm (4in)
SPREAD 30cm (12in)
SITE Full sun
SOIL Average, free-draining
HARDINESS Frost hardy
FLOWERING Summer

Chrysanthemum segetum Corn marigold

C

ONCE A COMMON WILDFLOWER, the corn marigold turned cornfields gold with its yellow, daisy-like flowers. It is now easy to grow this cheerful, long-flowering plant again because it is being included in most wildflower seed packets. If you live in a relatively mild region, sow the seeds in autumn in a greenhouse or on a windowsill for flowers in mid-spring. In colder regions, sow in spring where plants are to grow for summer flowers. Average, free-draining soil is fine.

OTHER VARIETIES 'Eastern Star' (primrose-yellow petals with a brown central disc); 'Prado' (golden-yellow petals with a contrasting dark brown centre).

PLANT PROFILE	
HEIGHT 80cm (32in)	
SPREAD 30cm (12in)	
SITE Full sun	
SOIL Average, free-draining	
HARDINESS Fully hardy	
FLOWERING Summer	

C | *Clarkia pulchella* Mixed Double Choice

CLARKIAS HAVE BEEN A BIG FAVOURITE since the Scottish plant hunter David Douglas collected some specimens in the 1820s (a few years later he fell into an animal trap on an island off Hawaii where he was gored to death by a bull who had also crashed in). The lilacs and pinks of Mixed Double Choice add a quiet, gentle touch to a flower border, and its parent, *C. pulchella*, is popular for its cut flowers. Sow the seeds in autumn or early spring where plants are to flower in slightly acid, moist but free-draining soil.

OTHER VARIETY 'Snowflake' (masses of pure white flowers).

PLANT PROFILE

HEIGHT 30cm (12in)

SPREAD 20cm (8in)

SITE Sun or partial shade

SOIL Slightly acid, average, moist but free-draining

HARDINESS Fully hardy

FLOWERING Summer

Clarkia 'Salmon Princess'

C

OFTEN LISTED AS GODETIA, the frilled and satiny flowers of 'Salmon Princess' are excellent for picking (remove the stems when the buds start fattening). Don't worry about spoiling the display, though, because individual flowers only last about one week and more will quickly appear. Sow the seeds in spring or autumn where plants are to flower, and grow in moist but free-draining, average but slightly acid soil that doesn't bake dry in summer.

OTHER VARIETIES *C. amoena* (fluted, single or double, lilac to red-pink flowers); Grace Series (single, lavender-pink, red, salmon-pink or pink flowers with contrasting centres).

PLANT PROFILE
HEIGHT 30cm (12in)
SPREAD 30cm (12in)
SITE Sun or partial shade
SOIL Slightly acid, average, moist but free-draining
HARDINESS Fully hardy
FLOWERING Summer

C | *Cleome hassleriana* 'Colour Fountain' **Spider flower**

THESE EYE-CATCHING, STIFF-STEMMED, chest-high annuals are topped by a colourful head of scented flowers, each with four upright petals. They add an exquisite dash to beds and borders when grown in bold groups of, say, six or more. The spider flower needs a warm summer to really flourish. For extra flowering branches, pinch off the growing tip but beware the short, sharp vicious spine where each leaf meets the stem. Sow the seeds in spring under glass, and grow in light, fertile, free-draining soil. To produce slightly shorter flowering plants for smaller beds, sow the seeds a little later in mid-spring.

OTHER VARIETY 'Helen Campbell' (clean white flowers).

PLANT PROFILE

HEIGHT 1.2m (4ft)

SPREAD 45cm (18in)

SITE Full sun

SOIL Light, fertile, free-draining

HARDINESS Min 4°C (39°F)

FLOWERING Midsummer to early autumn

Cobaea scandens Cathedral bell

C

A SPECTACULARLY VIGOROUS CLIMBER, easily capable of sprinting 4.5m (15ft) in its first summer, *C. scandens* produces fleshy, bell-shaped, scented flowers that open creamy-green and age to deep purple. The shape of its flowers and the stiff green sepals explains its other common name of cup and saucer vine. Choose the planting site with care because once the stems take off they latch onto anything in the way. Give it a clear run up a strong support, such as a sunny trellis, fence or wall with horizontal wires attached to it. In hot years, the flowers are followed by egg-shaped, inedible greenish fruit (*see inset*). Sow the seeds in spring on a warm windowsill or in a greenhouse, and grow in average, moist but free-draining soil.

PLANT PROFILE

HEIGHT 20m (70ft)

SITE Full sun

SOIL Average, moist but free-draining

HARDINESS Min 5°C (41°F)

FLOWERING Summer to autumn

PEARL-LIKE SEEDS

The hard, shiny seeds of Christ's tears ripen from green to pearly grey-purple. They are large and pretty enough to make into jewellery.

C | *Coix lacryma-jobi* Christ's tears

ANOTHER DESCRIPTIVE NAME FOR THIS PLANT would be necklace grass because the grain – which is only produced after a long, hot summer – is bead-like and tough enough for stringing into necklaces and rosaries. The best way to grow it is by sowing seed in early spring on a warm windowsill or in a greenhouse. Keep potting seedlings up into larger pots and then, when the outside summer temperatures are starting to warm up, plant them out at the foot of a sunny, sheltered wall where they can bask in the heat. Grow in light to medium soil that is fertile and moist but free-draining.

PLANT PROFILE

HEIGHT 90cm (36in)

SPREAD 30cm (12in)

SITE Full sun

SOIL Light to medium, fertile, moist but free-draining

HARDINESS Half hardy

FLOWERING Early autumn

Collinsia grandiflora

ALTHOUGH NOT AS WELL KNOWN as the widely available floppy *C. heterophylla* (still sometimes sold as *C. bicolor*), *C. grandiflora* deserves greater popularity on account of its pretty two-tone flowers. These consist of pale pink upper lips and blue-purple lower ones. Both plants, however, are well worth growing in borders and wild flower gardens (they need to be staked using twiggy sticks), and provide long-lasting cut flowers. Sow the seeds in early spring or autumn where plants are to flower in fertile, moist but free-draining soil in a sheltered site.

OTHER VARIETY *C. heterophylla* 'Candidissima' (pure white flowers).

PLANT PROFILE
HEIGHT 30cm (12in)
SPREAD 30cm (12in)
SITE Sun or partial shade
SOIL Fertile, moist but free-draining
HARDINESS Fully hardy
FLOWERING Spring to summer

C *Collinsia heterophylla* (syn. *C. bicolor*) Chinese houses

THE COMMON NAME, CHINESE HOUSES, was coined because each attractive bicoloured flower looks a bit like a Chinese pagoda. The flowers are tightly clustered together and encircle the slender, weak and floppy stems – they need strong support to ensure that the blooms are prevented from drooping. Sow the seeds in autumn or spring where the plants are to flower. The soil needs to be fertile and moist; flower production will be halted if it is allowed to dry out over summer. Once established it is a prolific self-seeder.

OTHER VARIETY 'Multicolor' (flowers marked white, lilac, and purple-pink).

PLANT PROFILE
HEIGHT 60cm (24in)
SPREAD 30cm (12in)
SITE Sun to partial shade
SOIL Fertile, moist but free-draining
HARDINESS Fully hardy
FLOWERING Spring to summer

Commelina coelestis Day flower

C

THE VIVID, PEACOCK BLUE FLOWERS of *C. coelestis* make it a valuable plant for most parts of the garden. The small flowers only last one day but there are always plenty more waiting to open. Sow the seeds in spring on a warm windowsill or in a greenhouse, and grow outdoors in fertile, free-draining soil. If the site is sheltered and mild, the frost-hardy day flower will survive outside over winter if covered with a protective mulch of bark chippings. Failing that, pop it in a pot and keep it in the greenhouse or on a windowsill ready for planting out the following spring after the last frost.

PLANT PROFILE
HEIGHT 90cm (36in)
SPREAD 45cm (18in)
SITE Sun or partial shade
SOIL Fertile, free-draining
HARDINESS Frost hardy
FLOWERING Late summer to mid-autumn

TOXIC SEEDS

The odd-looking seed pods of larkspur resemble small bat's ears, and contain poisonous seeds which, once collected, should be stored in a cool, dry place.

C

Consolida ajacis Giant Imperial Series Larkspur

THE LARKSPUR IS A FREE-AND-EASY cottage-garden plant that looks a bit like a delphinium. The Giant Imperial Series is earlier flowering and taller than most, with vertical spires of bright, double flowers that appear all summer and are good for cutting. The stems are stiff and straight, with branches appearing from low down. Sow the seeds in spring where they are to flower, and grow in light, fertile, free-draining soil, watering well in dry periods. Be sure to keep a look out for slugs and snails which can demolish the stems.

OTHER VARIETIES Dwarf Hyacinth Series (double, densely packed flowers); Dwarf Rocket Series (dwarf, compact, with double, blue, purple, white or pink flowers).

PLANT PROFILE
HEIGHT 100cm (36in)
SPREAD 35cm (14in)
SITE Full sun
SOIL Light, fertile, free-draining
HARDINESS Fully hardy
FLOWERING Summer

Convolvulus tricolor 'Royal Ensign' Bindweed

C

IF YOU WANT A SHORTER, BUSHIER, compact kind of ipomoea (morning glory), with a similar open flower and a brilliant blue colour, go for 'Royal Ensign' (ignore the common name, this is not a weed). Use it in hanging baskets or to fill gaps at the front of a border and in the rock garden. Short-lived flowers that open during the day, but close up at night, will keep appearing throughout summer. Sow the seeds in spring where flowers are to grow in poor to average, free-draining soil.

OTHER VARIETY Ensign Series (includes bright blue, pale blue, dark red, and rosy-red flowers).

PLANT PROFILE
HEIGHT 30cm (12in)
SPREAD 30cm (12in)
SITE Full sun
SOIL Poor to average, gritty, free-draining
HARDINESS Fully hardy
FLOWERING Summer

C | *Coreopsis grandiflora* 'Early Sunrise' Tickseed

GIVING A PROLIFIC SHOW of semi-double, pure yellow flowers, with a touch of orange near the centre, tickseed adds a flashy, summery touch to the garden. The stems are just the right height for the front of the border and mix well with reds and royal blues. Deadhead regularly to promote new flowers and to keep things looking tidy. Grow this perennial as an annual or biennial because it loses vigour after its first year. Sow the seeds in spring where plants are to flower, or in the summer for flowers the following year. Grow in fertile, free-draining soil.

OTHER VARIETIES 'Gold Star' (golden–yellow flowers and rolled or quilled petals); 'Sunray' (double, deep yellow flowers).

PLANT PROFILE

HEIGHT 45cm (18in)

SPREAD 45cm (18in)

SITE Full sun or partial shade

SOIL Fertile, free-draining

HARDINESS Fully hardy

FLOWERING Summer

Coreopsis tinctoria Tickseed

AN EXCELLENT INGREDIENT for summer borders, *C. tinctoria*'s small, bright yellow flowers have dark red eyes. It gives a terrific but not-too-overpowering lift where the colour scheme starts to sag, and is best mixed with rich blues and reds. The very finely divided, bright green leaves boost the display. Sow the seeds from early spring to early summer at regular intervals where plants are to flower. Grow in free-draining, fertile soil. To encourage flowering, keep snipping off blooms as they start to fade.

OTHER VARIETIES 'Mahogany Midget' (dwarf, with yellow and mahogany-scarlet flowers); 'Tiger Flower' (dwarf, with crimson to golden yellow flowers, many speckled and striped).

PLANT PROFILE
HEIGHT 1.2m (4ft)
SPREAD 45cm (18in)
SITE Full sun or partial shade
SOIL Fertile, free-draining
HARDINESS Fully hardy
FLOWERING Spring to autumn

C | *Coriandrum sativum* Coriander

YOU CAN GROW CORIANDER in north-west Europe, but for best results the plant really needs a long, hot summer. There are two options: *C. sativum* gives an equal supply of leaves and seed; while 'Cilantro' is best for an abundance of leaves. The tiny flowers are decorative, but it's the leaves and seeds that are used in oriental cooking (save unused seed for sowing the following year). With both types of coriander, wait until the light, free-draining soil has really warmed up in early summer before sowing; if sown any earlier, use a cloche to keep the ground warm. Support the lax stems with twiggy sticks to keep them upright.

OTHER VARIETY 'Cilantro' (more leaves than seed).

PLANT PROFILE
HEIGHT 50cm (20in)
SPREAD 20cm (8in)
SITE Full sun or partial shade
SOIL Light, fertile, free-draining
HARDINESS Fully hardy
FLOWERING Midsummer

Cosmos bipinnatus 'Sea Shells'

C

THERE ARE TWO GOOD REASONS for growing this plant. The first is its distinctive, yellow-eyed, open-petalled flowers, and the second is the fine, feathery foliage that makes an attractive, airy background. The flowers keep appearing all summer and put on a good show in border schemes, as well as making an excellent gap filler. Sow the seeds in mid-spring under glass, or sow a few weeks later where plants are to flower in average, moist but free-draining soil.

OTHER VARIETY 'Candy Stripe' (white flowers with a dark crimson margin, some flowers flecked with crimson, with the occasional pure crimson bloom).

PLANT PROFILE
HEIGHT 90cm (36in)
SPREAD 45cm (18in)
SITE Full sun
SOIL Average, moist but free-draining
HARDINESS Half hardy
FLOWERING Summer

C | *Cosmos sulphureus* Ladybird Series

IF YOU BUY VERY FEW PACKETS of seed, make one of them cosmos. The flowers are like small, open saucers with button eyes and are set off by the fine, feathery foliage. Ladybird plants have an abundance of long-lasting flowers, hairy stems (though the foliage is not as decorative as in other forms), and are short enough for the front of the border where they make excellent gap fillers. They also look good planted around features such as statues and clumps of lilies. Sow the seeds in mid-spring under glass, or sow a few weeks later where plants are to flower in average, moist but free-draining soil.

OTHER VARIETY 'Butterkist' (semi-double, yellow flowers).

PLANT PROFILE
HEIGHT 40cm (16in)
SPREAD 20cm (8in)
SITE Full sun
SOIL Average, moist but free-draining
HARDINESS Min 5°C (41°F)
FLOWERING Summer

Cotula coronopifolia Brass buttons

C

A RARE ANNUAL FOR A POND – where it is happy growing in shallow water, no more than 15cm (6in) deep – bog garden or damp border, the flowers of *C. coronopifolia* are small yellow discs or buttons (hence the common name) held on top of slender stalks. The fresh green leaves are up to 12cm (5in) long and strongly aromatic. A short-lived and slightly tender perennial, it is invariably best grown as an annual. Seed germinates easily (sprinkle it on top of the soil but don't cover it over) when sown in spring under glass. In borders it requires moist, fertile soil.

PLANT PROFILE	
HEIGHT	15cm (6in)
SPREAD	30cm (12in)
SITE	Full sun
SOIL	Moist, fertile
HARDINESS	Frost hardy
FLOWERING	Summer

C | *Crepis rubra* Hawk's beard

WELL WORTH GROWING FOR THE ARCHING STEMS that emerge from a ground-hugging rosette of leaves, hawk's beard also has small but long-lasting flowers. Keep picking them off as they fade and more will follow. Although it will survive the winter outside, the plant soon loses vigour, peters out and dies, and is best grown fresh each year as an annual. For a lovely ripple of white running through a planting of pink *C. rubra*, include equal numbers of the white *C. rubra* var. *alba*. Sow the seeds in autumn in a cold frame and plant out in free-draining soil. Once established it is a reliable self-seeder.

PLANT PROFILE

HEIGHT 40cm (16in)

SPREAD 15cm (6in)

SITE Full sun

SOIL Free-draining

HARDINESS Fully hardy

FLOWERING Spring to summer

Cuphea llavea 'Tiny Mice'

C

SMALL AND SHRUBBY, 'TINY MICE' is easily recognized by its short flower stems with leaves opposite each other. At the base of each bloom there is a touch of purple which has been likened to a Mickey Mouse face with two black ears. *C.* x *purpurea* grows about twice as tall, and has pink to red flowers. Sow the seeds in early spring under glass, or a few weeks later where plants are to flower. Both like free-draining, average soil.

OTHER VARIETIES *C. hyssopifolia* (light pink-purple, pink or white flowers); *C. ignea* (deep red flowers, each with a dark red band, a white trim and two tiny black-purple petals).

PLANT PROFILE
HEIGHT 23cm (9in)
SPREAD 15cm (6in)
SITE Full sun or partial shade
SOIL Average, free-draining
HARDINESS Half hardy
FLOWERING Spring to autumn

C | *Cuphea* x *purpurea* 'Firefly'

THE PARENTAGE OF THIS BUSHY ANNUAL goes back to the tropical and sub-tropical Americas, making it a lively ingredient for a hothouse border. The flowers keep appearing right through summer above the dark green leaves, at the very top of the stems. To overwinter the plant, dig it up, pot it in a container and keep it in the conservatory – in time it will eventually become quite shrubby. Alternatively, sow the seeds each year in early spring under glass, or a few weeks later where plants are to flower, in average, free-draining soil.

OTHER VARIETY 'Avalon' (purple flowers).

PLANT PROFILE	
HEIGHT 60cm (24in)	
SPREAD 45cm (18in)	
SITE Full sun or partial shade	
SOIL Average, free-draining	
HARDINESS Half hardy	
FLOWERING Spring to autumn	

Cynoglossum amabile 'Firmament' Chinese forget-me-not

C

WITH ITS SPRAYS OF INTENSE BLUE FLOWERS (which are sometimes white or pale pink with white or blue eyes), this annual or biennial is best grown in groups (a massed effect is essential) weaving along the front of a border or around shrubs. Though it can be grown as a summer annual, you will get better results by sowing the seed in early autumn where the plants are to flower the following spring. Grow in moist but free-draining, slightly fertile soil – avoid over-fertile ground which gives poor results.

OTHER VARIETY 'Mystery Rose' (off-white flowers with a touch of pink or lilac).

PLANT PROFILE
HEIGHT 40cm (16in)
SPREAD 30cm (12in)
SITE Sun or partial shade
SOIL Average, moist but free-draining
HARDINESS Fully hardy
FLOWERING Spring to early summer

D | *Dahlia* Coltness Hybrids

WITH THEIR EXQUISITE COLOURS and the ease with which they can be raised, the advantage of growing a dahlia as an annual is that the plant can be thrown away at the end of autumn. Grown as a perennial, its underground cluster of potato-like tubers must be dug up and stored over winter. If you have a favourite seed-grown dahlia that you want to keep for next year, store the tubers in a big pot of lightly dampened, coarse vermiculite in a frost-free place. Sow the seeds in early spring under glass, and grow outdoors in fertile, free-draining soil and feed with tomato fertilizer in summer.

OTHER VARIETY 'Figaro' (double, sometimes semi-double flowers in mixed colours including white, yellow, red, and pink).

PLANT PROFILE

HEIGHT 45cm (18in)

SPREAD 45cm (18in)

SITE Full sun

SOIL Fertile, free-draining

HARDINESS Half hardy

FLOWERING Midsummer to autumn

Delphinium nudicaule

A SHORT-LIVED PERENNIAL, this plant needs to be grown as an annual. The funnel-shaped flowers in bright red, orange-red or yellow have red to yellow throats and appear on sturdy, upright stems. The new cultivar, *D. nudicaule* 'Laurin' – a miniature at just 38cm (15in) tall – is well worth growing for its multi-branching stems and long-lasting, orange-red blooms. It flowers within five months of seed sowing, and can be used in pots or at the front of a border. Sow the seeds in early spring under glass, and plant out in fertile, free-draining soil. Given a chance, slugs and snails will strip the stems.

OTHER VARIETY *D. cardinale* (elf cap-shaped, stout-spurred, single scarlet flowers).

PLANT PROFILE

HEIGHT 60cm (24in)

SPREAD 20cm (8in)

SITE Full sun

SOIL Fertile, free-draining

HARDINESS Fully hardy

FLOWERING Midsummer

D | *Delphinium requienii*

AN INTRIGUINGLY DIFFERENT DELPHINIUM with glossy leaves and an early summer display of flowers, this is not as showy as some varieties and looks best in quiet, pastel colour schemes. It comes from southern France and Sardinia, and will thrive in long, hot, dry summers. When growing it as an annual, sow the seeds either in winter or spring in a cold frame, or for flowers the following year sow the seeds at the start of summer. Grow in fertile, free-draining soil, and beware slugs and snails which are a dreadful menace.

OTHER VARIETY *D. grandiflorum* (elf cap-shaped, single, blue, violet and white flowers).

PLANT PROFILE

HEIGHT 100cm (39in)

SPREAD 45cm (18in)

SITE Full sun

SOIL Fertile, free-draining

HARDINESS Fully hardy

FLOWERING Early summer

Dianthus barbatus Monarch Series Sweet William

D

PACKED WITH SMALL FRAGRANT FLOWERS, sweet William can be grown as a short-lived perennial or, more typically, as a biennial. Traditionally grown in cottage gardens, the plants make an effective combination with groups of tulips but they can look good arranged in formal blocks. The best time to sow the seeds is in mid-spring in a cold frame, ready for planting out in autumn to flower the following year. Grow in average, free-draining soil. Once established the plant will readily self-seed.

OTHER VARIETIES 'Indian Carpet' (crimson, purple or pink flowers, many bicolours); 'Wee Willie' (crimson, rose-pink or white flowers).

PLANT PROFILE
HEIGHT 60cm (24in)
SPREAD 30cm (12in)
SITE Full sun
SOIL Neutral to alkaline, free-draining
HARDINESS Fully hardy
FLOWERING Late spring and early summer

Rather than buying packets of sweet William seeds, collect your own from the garden. Germination is quick, usually within ten days of sowing.

D

Dianthus barbatus Nigrescens Group Sweet William

THE NIGRESCENS SWEET WILLIAMS ARE just as good as the Monarch Series, and the same points apply, except that these have deep, rich red flowers and dark stems. Grow them in any gaps at the front of a border or, for a bright, punchy display, among groups of white tulips. The best time to sow the seeds is in mid-spring in a cold frame, planting outdoors in autumn in average, free-draining soil. The plants will be ready to flower the following year. In future years, the plants will self-seed.

OTHER VARIETY Roundabout Series (bushy, in a range of single colours and bicolours).

PLANT PROFILE

HEIGHT 60cm (24in)

SPREAD 25cm (10in)

SITE Full sun

SOIL Neutral to alkaline, free-draining

HARDINESS Fully hardy

FLOWERING Late spring and early summer

Dianthus caryophyllus Knight Series Wild carnation

D

THE BEST THREE CLOVE-SCENTED cultivars of *D. caryophyllus* are the Knight Series, Chabaud Giant and Floristan Series. Knight Series offers a range of bright colours and double flowers on small, bushy, multi-branching plants. Chabaud – taller, at 45cm (18in) high – has large, double flowers in a range of colours, and the 60cm (24in) tall Floristan was specially bred for the cut-flower market. Sow these last two in mid-spring for flowering the following year. Sow the seeds of the Knight Series in late winter or early spring under glass, and plant out into free-draining soil.

OTHER VARIETY Lillipot Series (double flowers in lavender-pink, purple, yellow, scarlet, and orange, some bicolours).

PLANT PROFILE	
HEIGHT 30cm (12in)	
SPREAD 23cm (9in)	
SITE Full sun	
SOIL Neutral to alkaline, free-draining	
HARDINESS Fully hardy	
FLOWERING Summer	

D **_Dianthus chinensis_ Ideal Series Chinese pink**

THE FLOWERS OF THESE SHORT-LIVED PERENNIALS come in a range
of colours, including bright crimson-red, and some are flushed with a
second colour. You must keep removing fading flowers to encourage
more buds to form. With a few exceptions, most fully hardy dianthus
prefer light, neutral to alkaline soil that is free-draining – mix in
plenty of horticultural grit if drainage needs improving. If your
garden soil is solid, heavy and lumpy, consider growing plants in a
specially prepared raised bed or a large container. Sow the seeds in
late winter or early spring under glass.

OTHER VARIETIES 'Fire Carpet' (scarlet flowers); 'Parfait' (lightly
fringed flowers, some with bicolours).

PLANT PROFILE
HEIGHT 35cm (14in)
SPREAD 23cm (9in)
SITE Full sun
SOIL Neutral to alkaline, free-draining
HARDINESS Fully hardy
FLOWERING Summer

Digitalis grandiflora Yellow foxglove

D

THIS FOXGLOVE HAS PALE YELLOW FLOWERS, and is a short-lived perennial that will thrive in the dappled shade of cottage-style borders and at the edge of woodland sites. The tubular flowers have conspicuous brown veins and are grouped in clusters above the leaves. Once established, it will self-seed and the resultant seedlings are easily dug up in spring and placed where you want them to grow. Sow the seeds in late summer and autumn to flower the following year. Grow in almost any soil except very wet or very dry, although most foxgloves do prefer it to be rich in leafmould.

OTHER VARIETY *D. lanata* (pale cream or fawn flowers).

PLANT PROFILE
HEIGHT 1m (3ft)
SPREAD 45cm (18in)
SITE Partial shade
SOIL Average
HARDINESS Fully hardy
FLOWERING Early to midsummer

D | *Digitalis purpurea* f. *albiflora* Common foxglove

A TOWERING SPIRE OF WHITE, TUBULAR FLOWERS arranged around a sturdy stem – except for the lower part where the long, green leaves stick out horizontally – makes this a dramatic plant for the cottage garden or woodland edge. For more colour, try the Excelsior Group which comes in purple, pink, yellow, and white, and makes spectacular drifts. Once established (it is actually a short-lived perennial), it will self-seed around the garden. Sow the seeds *in situ* in late summer and autumn to flower the following year, and grow in almost any soil.

OTHER VARIETY 'Gloxinioides' (frilly margined flowers in salmon-pink, cream-yellow, purple or pink).

PLANT PROFILE

HEIGHT 2m (6ft)

SPREAD 60cm (24in)

SITE Partial shade

SOIL Average

HARDINESS Fully hardy

FLOWERING Early summer

Digitalis purpurea Foxy Group Common foxglove

THE PASTEL-COLOURED AMERICAN FOXGLOVES have the advantage of being shorter than the traditional, self-seeding varieties, and work particularly well when grouped together in the middle of the border. The heavily spotted flowers on vertical spires are essential ingredients in cottage gardens or close to trees. The short-lived *D. purpurea* and its cultivars flower best in their first summer and need to be grown as biennials. Sow the seeds of the Foxy Group in late winter under glass to flower the following summer. Damp shade is fine, as is almost any soil, but avoid extremes.

OTHER VARIETY 'Sutton's Apricot' (apricot-pink flowers).

PLANT PROFILE	
HEIGHT 90cm (36in)	
SPREAD 60cm (24in)	
SITE Partial shade	
SOIL Average	
HARDINESS Fully hardy	
FLOWERING Early summer	

D | *Dimorphotheca pluvialis* Rain daisy

LOOKING JUST LIKE AN OSTEOSPERMUM, *D. pluvialis* has large, daisy-like flowers with white petals surrounding a violet-brown disc, and dark green leaves. When everything else is flagging during a long, dry spell, it keeps on performing. Grow it in rock gardens, gaps in patio paving or to the front of a border. The flowers close on overcast days, hence the common name of rain daisy. Sow the seeds in early spring under glass, or a few weeks later where plants are to flower. In its native South Africa, the plant grows in hot, dry, light, free-draining soil, and that is just what it needs in the garden.

OTHER VARIETIES 'Glistening White' (white flowers, tinged violet); 'Tetra Polar Star' (white flowers with deep violet-blue central discs).

PLANT PROFILE	
HEIGHT	40cm (16in)
SPREAD	30cm (12in)
SITE	Full sun
SOIL	Free-draining
HARDINESS	Half hardy
FLOWERING	Summer

Dipsacus fullonum Teasel

D

THE VERTICAL STEMS OF THE TEASEL are well protected by sharp prickles and the long spiny leaves that form in pairs along its length. Rainwater collects in the hollow where each leaf meets the stem. It is a valuable wildlife plant: the cone at the top is made up of tiny flowers that attract bees, while the later seedheads provide a food source for birds. Leave the stem and flower to add shape to the winter garden, or use in dried-flower arrangements. Sow the seeds in autumn where plants are to flower the following year, and grow in any soil, including clay. The teasel is an excellent self-seeder.

PLANT PROFILE

HEIGHT 2m (6ft)

SPREAD 80cm (32in)

SITE Sun or partial shade

SOIL Average

HARDINESS Fully hardy

FLOWERING Mid- and late summer

D *Dorotheanthus bellidiformis* Livingstone daisy

THESE DAISY-LIKE FLOWERS, which close when it is overcast, measure about 4cm (1½in) across, and are excellent gap fillers for the front of borders. The blooms have dark eyes and sometimes a contrasting ring of colour around the base of the petals. Packets of seed usually offer a mix of different colours to guarantee a lively display. Sow the seeds in late winter or early spring under glass, and plant out in poor, light, free-draining soil.

OTHER VARIETIES 'Lunette' (soft yellow flowers with a red centre); 'Magic Carpet' (pink, purple, cream, orange or white flowers).

PLANT PROFILE
HEIGHT 15cm (6in)
SPREAD 30cm (12in)
SITE Full sun
SOIL Poor, free-draining
HARDINESS Half hardy
FLOWERING Summer

Downingia elegans Blue calico flower

D

IN ITS NATIVE NORTH AMERICA, the trailing or mat-forming blue calico flower is found growing in damp ditches and wet areas, and needs similar garden conditions to thrive. The outer fringes of a bog garden are an obvious home for it, although if you can be diligent about keeping the compost damp, it will also grow well in a hanging basket or container. Take care when choosing planting companions lest they swamp this pretty plant with its lobelia-like, white-eyed, purplish flowers. Sow the seeds in late winter on a warm windowsill or in a heated greenhouse, or sow in spring where plants are to flower.

PLANT PROFILE
HEIGHT 15cm (6in)
SPREAD 15cm (6in)
SITE Sun or partial shade
SOIL Moist but free-draining
HARDINESS Fully hardy
FLOWERING Summer

D | *Dracocephalum moldavica* Dragon's head

DRAGON'S HEAD IS AN UNUSUAL PLANT with hooded, two-lipped summer flowers that attract bees. Crush the grey-green leaves between your fingers and you will detect the tangy scent of lemon. Standing erect and bushy, *D. moldavica* is a good gap filler in gravel gardens or borders with good drainage, but it will need some shade from the midday sun. Sow the seeds in mid-spring where plants are to grow, in average garden soil.

PLANT PROFILE

HEIGHT 60cm (24in)

SPREAD 30cm (12in)

SITE Full sun

SOIL Average, free-draining

HARDINESS Fully hardy

FLOWERING Summer

Eccremocarpus scaber Anglia Hybrids Chilean glory vine

E

IN ITS FIRST YEAR, A BAD WINTER could kill this frost-hardy evergreen, although it will survive outdoors in milder weather. It is, however, best treated as an annual climber in north-west Europe, guaranteeing a great upsurge of leafy, scrambling growth and tendrils that grab anything in the way. The clusters of flowers are like miniature waxy bottles (followed by inflated seed pods), and the bright colours add plenty of pizzazz. One way to limit the height of this plant is to sow the seeds under glass in spring rather than in late winter, thereby giving it less time to grow. Plant it in fertile, free-draining soil, and provide a hedge, pergola or wires against a wall for support.

OTHER VARIETY *E. scaber.* f. *roseus* (bright pink to light red flowers).

PLANT PROFILE

HEIGHT 3m (10ft)

SPREAD Indefinite

SITE Full sun

SOIL Fertile, free-draining

HARDINESS Frost hardy

FLOWERING Summer to autumn

E | *Echium vulgare* Viper's bugloss

VIPER'S BUGLOSS IS A COLOURFUL early summer plant that carries masses of blue (sometimes pink or white) flowers on its upright, tangled stems. It makes a lively contribution to wildflower gardens where bees and butterflies will home in on its blooms. *E. vulgare* is a medium-sized plant – if you're looking for something shorter choose a dwarf hybrid at 45cm (18in) tall with pink, purple, lilac-blue or white flowers. Sow the seeds in summer under glass, and plant outdoors the following spring in average, free-draining soil.

OTHER VARIETY 'Blue Bedder' (shorter, light blue flowers, ageing to bluish-pink).

PLANT PROFILE

HEIGHT 90cm (36in)

SPREAD 30cm (12in)

SITE Full sun

SOIL Average, free-draining

HARDINESS Fully hardy

FLOWERING Early summer

Echium wildpretii

E

BEES AND BUTTERFLIES ADORE ECHIUMS and will soon seek out the flowers in your garden. This type is a short-lived perennial from the Canary Islands, where it grows on stony hillsides and produces extraordinary columns packed with tiny, funnel-shaped flowers. Sow the seeds in late summer in pots on a warm windowsill or in a greenhouse, and plant outdoors the following spring. Grow in average, free-draining soil in a cottage garden or mixed border.

OTHER VARIETY *E. candicans* (white, blue-white or deep purple-blue flowers).

PLANT PROFILE
HEIGHT 2m (6ft)
SPREAD 60cm (24in)
SITE Full sun
SOIL Average, free-draining
HARDINESS Half hardy
FLOWERING Late spring to summer

E

Emilia coccinea Flora's paintbrush

A PROLIFIC, SELF-SOWING ANNUAL, *E. coccinea* produces stems of small, colourful, paintbrush-shaped blooms that rise out of a rosette of leaves. In the garden the plant is a little too dainty and almost weed-like to make much impact, but a group grown for cutting and drying never disappoints. Each plant has a long flowering period, especially if you keep removing dead blooms. *E. sonchifolia* does not flower nearly as well but has equally colourful flowers. Sow the seeds in mid-spring in pots on a warm windowsill or in a greenhouse, and plant outdoors in average, free-draining soil.

OTHER VARIETY *E. sonchifolia* (fluffy, purple-red flowers).

PLANT PROFILE

HEIGHT 60cm (24in)

SPREAD 60cm (24in)

SITE Full sun

SOIL Average, free-draining

HARDINESS Half hardy

FLOWERING Summer

Erigeron karvinskianus 'Profusion' Fleabane

E

A TINY, MUTICOLOURED DAISY, *E. karvinskianus* is the parent plant of 'Profusion' and has white petals with a yellow eye – the white then ages to pink and purple, so that at any one moment there are three different colours in a group of plants. 'Profusion' has pink or white flowers. Both plants are spreading in nature and typically grown in cracks in paving and walls, which they quickly colonize, and where they immediately stand out. Once established they keep flowering every year. Sow in mid- or late spring in a cold frame, and plant out in free-draining soil where there is some shade at midday.

OTHER VARIETIES *E. aureus* (deep golden-yellow flowers); *E. chrysopsidis* 'Grand Ridge' (masses of deep yellow flowers).

PLANT PROFILE	
HEIGHT 30cm (12in)	
SPREAD 50cm (20in)	
SITE Full sun	
SOIL Free-draining	
HARDINESS Fully hardy	
FLOWERING Summer	

E

Erysimum cheiri Bedder Series Wallflower

ONE OF THE BEST SPRING PLANTS, the short-lived wallflower has rich and warm flower colours with a surprisingly sweet scent. The compact Bedder Series can be grown together in bold groups or used in a classic combination among clumps of tulips – trim after flowering. Even better, grow them in walls because they thrive on free-draining soil. Sow the seeds from late spring to early summer outdoors in a spare (non-acid) bed, and move to their final positions in mid-autumn ready for flowering the following year.

OTHER VARIETIES 'Blood Red' (deep red flowers); 'Fire King' (orange-red flowers); 'Ivory White' (creamy-white flowers).

PLANT PROFILE

HEIGHT 30cm (12in)

SPREAD 30cm (12in)

SITE Full sun

SOIL Neutral or alkaline, free-draining

HARDINESS Fully hardy

FLOWERING Spring

Eschscholzia caespitosa California poppy

 E

OUT OF AN UNPREPOSSESSING TUFT of finely divided leaves come short flower stems holding bright yellow, cupped, faintly scented flowers. To make sure that *E. caespitosa* is seen clearly, plant it in gravel or rock gardens, or in gaps in paving, but wherever it is grown, ensure it gets plenty of bright sun. Sow the seeds in spring or autumn where plants are to flower, in poor, free-draining soil.

PLANT PROFILE	
HEIGHT 15cm (6in)	
SPREAD 15cm (6in)	
SITE Full sun	
SOIL Poor, free-draining	
HARDINESS Fully hardy	
FLOWERING Summer	

OTHER VARIETY 'Sundew' (lemon-yellow flowers).

BIRD BARRIER

Birds love the seed of the California poppy, so protect it under chicken wire – this will also provide support for emerging seedlings.

E

Eschscholzia californica California poppy

IF YOU ARE NERVOUS ABOUT GROWING ANNUALS, these poppies could not be easier. Scatter the seeds on the ground in spring where they are to flower, and with a bit of sun and rain up pop slender stems topped by delicate, paper-thin petals, surrounded by finely cut leaves. Grow them in groups for maximum impact, to run in ripples through a border or under apple trees – in fact, on any spare patch of ground. All they need is poor soil and good drainage.

OTHER VARIETY 'Ballerina' (fluted, semi-double or double, red, pink, yellow or orange flowers).

PLANT PROFILE

HEIGHT 30cm (12in)

SPREAD 15cm (6in)

SITE Full sun

SOIL Poor, free-draining

HARDINESS Fully hardy

FLOWERING Summer

Euphorbia lathyris Caper spurge

E

IF YOU HAVE BEEN TOLD this plant wards off moles… sorry, it's not true. But there is one very good reason for growing the caper spurge between cracks in paving or in gravel gardens (or anywhere with light, free-draining soil): it has a fun, quirky shape. The erect stems have leathery, waxy, grey to blue-green leaves, about 15cm (6in) long, and the small summer flowers are followed by green, caper-like fruit – in turn, two stems shoot out beside the fruit which then flower and fruit. Viewed from close-up, it is a gem. Sow the seeds in spring under glass for flowering the following year.

OTHER VARIETY *E. cyathophora* (scarlet and green bracts).

PLANT PROFILE
HEIGHT 1.2m (4ft)
SPREAD 30cm (12in)
SITE Full sun
SOIL Light, free-draining
HARDINESS Fully hardy
FLOWERING Summer

E

Euphorbia marginata Ghost weed

COMING LARGELY FROM MEXICO and the Rocky Mountains in North America, *E. marginata* has become immensely popular (particularly with florists as a cut flower) for its green and white variegated leaves. They are larger at the bottom of the plant than up at the top, where they become progressively smaller. Ghost weed looks good with the tomato red *Crocosmia* 'Lucifer' and blue agapanthus. Sow the seeds in spring where the plants are to flower, in light, free-draining soil.

OTHER VARIETY *E. portlandica* (grey-tinged, bright green leaves).

PLANT PROFILE

HEIGHT 90cm (36in)

SPREAD 30cm (12in)

SITE Full sun

SOIL Light, free-draining

HARDINESS Fully hardy

FLOWERING Late summer to autumn

Eustoma grandiflorum Yodel Series **Texan bluebell**

E

THIS NORTH AMERICAN PRAIRIE PLANT was initially sold in north-west Europe as a house plant, but is now used as a dashing summer annual. It also makes an excellent cut flower. Yodel Series cultivars are compact with broadly bell-shaped, satin-textured flowers in white, salmon-pink or purple-blue with dark centres. For really small plants, try the 15cm (6in) high Mermaid Series with its pink-, white-, or black-centred blue flowers. Sow the seeds in autumn or late winter under glass, and grow outdoors in free-draining, neutral to alkaline soil.

OTHER VARIETY Heidi Series (flowers in shades of blue, rose-pink, white, and bicolours).

PLANT PROFILE
HEIGHT 45cm (16–18in)
SPREAD 23cm (9in)
SITE Full sun
SOIL Neutral to alkaline, free-draining
HARDINESS Min 5–7°C (41–45°F)
FLOWERING Summer

E

Exacum affine Persian violet

TYPICALLY GROWN AS A CONSERVATORY or house plant for its richly scented flowers, each with a yellow centre, the Persian violet can also be grown outside in summer. Bushy and compact, with shiny leaves, the flowers add a lovely touch to the garden but to appreciate the scent fully, grow them in containers – this means it's easy to move them around, keeping them in the sun. Sow the seeds in early spring under glass, and grow in average, free-draining soil.

OTHER VARIETIES 'Blue Gem' (shorter, lavender-blue flowers); 'Blue Midget' (shorter, lavender-blue flowers); 'White Midget' (pure white flowers).

PLANT PROFILE

HEIGHT 30cm (12in)

SPREAD 30cm (12in)

SITE Full sun

SOIL Average, free-draining

HARDINESS Min 7–10°C (45–50°F)

FLOWERING Summer

Felicia amelloides Blue daisy

THESE SOUTH AFRICAN DAISIES make a beautiful summery show in rock or gravel gardens, at the front of borders, encircling a pond or in containers. Each plant produces a prolific show of yellow–centred flowers. 'Santa Anita' is a popular rich blue, while 'Santa Anita Variegated' has leaves with attractive white markings. Sow the seeds in spring under glass, and plant out in poor to average, free-draining soil in full sun. Plants can be dug up in autumn and overwintered in pots in the conservatory, ready for flowering the following summer, or you can simply discard them and buy new plants each year.

OTHER VARIETIES *F. bergeriana* (brilliant clear blue flowers with yellow centres); *F. heterophylla* (blue flowers).

PLANT PROFILE
HEIGHT 60cm (24in)
SPREAD 60cm (24in)
SITE Full sun
SOIL Poor to average
HARDINESS Min 3°C (37°F)
FLOWERING Summer to autumn

F

Fuchsia 'Florabelle'

THE LAX, BRANCHING, FLOWERING STEMS of 'Florabelle' cascade wonderfully over the sides of hanging baskets, or from the rims of tall, Victorian chimney pots, or raised beds. Extremely free-flowering, its dark tones are just right for those who hate fuchsias in flamboyant sugar pink. A half-hardy plant, it can be dug up in autumn and kept in a conservatory over winter for planting out early the following summer. Sow the seeds in spring under glass for flowers in four months; plant out in fertile, moist but free-draining soil.

OTHER VARIETY 'Cascade' (white, carmine-red and deep carmine-red flowers).

PLANT PROFILE

HEIGHT 60cm (24in)

SPREAD 45cm (18in)

SITE Full sun or partial shade

SOIL Moist but free-draining

HARDINESS Half hardy

FLOWERING Summer

Fuchsia procumbens Trailing fuchsia

A NATIVE OF NEW ZEALAND, *F. procumbens* is very different from the typical flowery, cheery pink kind of fuchsia. The flowers are colourful and an unusual shape: the short tube is greenish-yellow to pale orange with a touch of red at the base, the turned-backed sepals are purple, and the stamens carry bright blue pollen. The small, upward-facing blooms emerge in summer against a backdrop of horizontal stems and rounded, heart-shaped leaves. The best feature is the plum-sized, bright red fruits. Sow the seeds in spring under glass and plant out in fertile, moist but free-draining soil. In mild areas, this fuchsia will do well in a rock or gravel garden.

OTHER VARIETY *F.* 'Red Spider' (crimson and rose-red flowers).

PLANT PROFILE
HEIGHT 15cm (6in)
SPREAD 1.2m (4ft)
SITE Full sun or partial shade
SOIL Moist but free-draining
HARDINESS Frost hardy (borderline)
FLOWERING Summer to autumn

G | *Gaillardia* x *grandiflora* 'Kobold' Blanket flower

A PUNCHY, FLAMBOYANT, SHORT-LIVED perennial that is commonly grown as an annual. The flowers of 'Kobold' have yellow-tipped red petals with a dark red centre. Definitely not for the timid, it is worth growing to fill gaps in the border where the colour scheme needs a boost. The flowers are about 10cm (4in) wide, and are good for cutting. Sow the seeds in early spring under glass, and grow in light, free-draining soil.

OTHER VARIETIES 'Burgunder' (deep wine-red flowers); 'Dazzler' (flashy orange-red, yellow-tipped petals and maroon centre).

PLANT PROFILE
HEIGHT 30cm (12in)
SPREAD 30cm (12in)
SITE Full sun
SOIL Light, free-draining
HARDINESS Fully hardy
FLOWERING Early summer to early autumn

Gaillardia pulchella 'Lollipops' Blanket flower

G

THE NORTH AMERICAN COMMON NAME of this plant is firewheels, which gives a good description of its colour combination: red and yellow around a dark centre. Group plants together to give a mass of flowers all summer. 'Lollipops' is bushy, upright and branching, and its flowers appear above grey-green leaves. Sow the seeds in early spring on a warm windowsill or in a greenhouse, and grow outdoors in light, free-draining soil.

OTHER VARIETY 'Portola Giants' (slightly larger, bronze-scarlet, gold-tipped flowers).

PLANT PROFILE
HEIGHT 30cm (12in)
SPREAD 30cm (12in)
SITE Full sun
SOIL Light, free-draining
HARDINESS Fully hardy
FLOWERING Spring to autumn

G | *Gazania* Chansonette Series

PACKED WITH COLOURFUL FLOWER POWER, these South African daisies appear on top of erect, slender stems. The long, glossy leaves are dark green on top and covered with white, silky hairs underneath. Since they need very good drainage they are ideal in rock, gravel, and Mediterranean-type gardens, as well as in containers. Sow the seeds in late winter or early spring under glass, and plant out in light, sandy soil.

OTHER VARIETIES Daybreak Series (bronze, orange, yellow, bright pink or white flowers, usually zoned in a contrasting colour); Talent Series (slightly taller, more vigorous).

PLANT PROFILE

HEIGHT 20cm (8in)

SPREAD 25cm (10in)

SITE Full sun

SOIL Light, sandy, free-draining

HARDINESS Half hardy

FLOWERING Summer

Gilia capitata Queen Anne's thimbles

G

MOST GILIAS ARE FROM THE DESERT AREAS of the southern states of North America. Given a suitably sunny site and light, free-draining soil, they make a lovely display with their small, fluffy pincushion flowers in a range of colours, including violet, pink or red. The blooms are set off by bright green, feathery leaves. This delicate-looking plant deserves to be much more popular in cottage gardens. Sow the seeds in autumn or mid-spring where plants are to flower, or sow in early spring in pots on a warm windowsill or greenhouse.

OTHER VARIETY *G. achilleifolia* (mid-blue to violet-blue flowers).

PLANT PROFILE	
HEIGHT 60cm (24in)	
SPREAD 23cm (9in)	
SITE Full sun	
SOIL Light, free-draining	
HARDINESS Fully hardy	
FLOWERING Summer	

G Gilia tricolor Bird's eyes

CHOCOLATE-SCENTED AND SAUCER-SHAPED, the small flowers of
G. tricolor have orange or yellow centres, with light blue around the
rims. The plants form mounds of finely divided, bright green leaves,
and look best when grown in small groups in gaps in patio paving,
or on dry, sunny banks. Sow the seeds in autumn or mid-spring
where plants are to flower, or sow in early spring in pots on a
windowsill or in a greenhouse and plant outdoors in light, free-
draining soil.

PLANT PROFILE

HEIGHT 45cm (18in)

SPREAD 23cm (9in)

SITE Full sun

SOIL Light, free-draining

HARDINESS Fully hardy

FLOWERING Late spring
to late summer

Glaucium corniculatum Red horned poppy

G

IF YOU ARE LOOKING FOR an extra colourful ingredient for a gravel garden or cracks between paving (where there is excellent drainage), the red-horned poppy, with its loose clusters of small, saucer-shaped flowers, creates a very beautiful effect. Leave a few flowers to develop seedheads to provide more plants the following year, and keep snipping off the rest as they fade for a long succession of flowers throughout the summer. Sow the seeds in autumn where plants are to flower in poor to average, free-draining soil.

PLANT PROFILE

HEIGHT 40cm (16in)

SPREAD 40cm (16in)

SITE Full sun

SOIL Free-draining

HARDINESS Fully hardy

FLOWERING Summer to early autumn

G | *Glaucium flavum* Yellow horned poppy

GROWN FOR ITS BRIGHT POPPY-LIKE FLOWERS, *G. flavum* is a rosette-forming, short-lived perennial that is usually grown as a biennial. Its rough, hairless, blue-green leaves are incised or toothed, and it produces branched grey stems of bright golden-yellow or orange flowers in summer. Native to Europe, the Canary Islands, North Africa and West Asia, glauciums should be grown in poor to average, sharply drained soil, and their seeds sown in spring or autumn where the plants are to flower.

PLANT PROFILE

HEIGHT 90cm (36in)

SPREAD 45cm (18in)

SITE Full sun

SOIL Very free-draining

HARDINESS Fully hardy

FLOWERING Summer

Gomphrena 'Strawberry Fields'

G

IF YOU'RE LOOKING FOR A PLANT that will thrive in a long, hot summer and show no sign of flagging, go for gomphrenas. 'Strawberry Fields' forms a clump of upright stems topped by cone-like shapes, each cone made up of dozens of tiny flowers which can be cut for dried-flower arrangements (they will retain their bright colour). Sow the seeds in early spring under glass, and make sure that the plants get the sunniest position in the garden and average, free-draining soil.

OTHER VARIETY *G. globosa* 'Buddy' (vivid, deep purple flowers).

PLANT PROFILE

HEIGHT 80cm (32in)

SPREAD 30cm (12in)

SITE Full sun

SOIL Average, free-draining

HARDINESS Half hardy

FLOWERING Summer to early autumn

G | *Gypsophila elegans*

GOOD VALUE, FLOWER-PACKED AND SPRAWLING, *G. elegans* makes a billowing spray of flowers, sometimes with pink or purple veins. The airy, fuzzy effect, like thousands of hovering insects, works well in cottage gardens in front of bright red perennials. Since the display is quite short, sow the seeds in three or four batches at 14-day intervals to prolong the show. Sow the first seed batch in spring where plants are to flower, with subsequent sowings in pots if they are for the same position. Grow in light, preferably alkaline, fast-draining soil.

OTHER VARIETIES 'Carminea' (deep carmine-pink flowers); 'Covent Garden' (large white flowers); 'Red Cloud' (carmine-pink flowers).

PLANT PROFILE

HEIGHT 60cm (24in)

SPREAD 30cm (12in)

SITE Full sun

SOIL Preferably alkaline, light, very free-draining

HARDINESS Fully hardy

FLOWERING Summer

BIRD SEED

As with all sunflowers, it is a good idea to leave the dead flowerheads on the plants as their seeds are an important food source for birds in winter.

Helianthus annuus 'Music Box' Sunflower

H

A NOVEL SUNFLOWER, 'MUSIC BOX' does not have a lamppost-like stem with a gigantic face perched high in the sky, but is a multi-branching, thigh-high bushy plant. It produces dozens of 10cm (4in) wide flowers, and plants come in a range of colours, including some bicoloured, but all have a black disc in the centre. Sow the seeds in spring where plants are to flower, but beware of pigeons tucking into them in the morning like muesli. Grow them in average, neutral to alkaline, free-draining soil.

OTHER VARIETY 'Autumn Beauty' (dark mahogany-red, lemon-yellow, golden-yellow or bronze-red petals).

PLANT PROFILE
HEIGHT 70cm (28in)
SPREAD 60cm (24in)
SITE Full sun
SOIL Neutral to alkaline, average, moist but free-draining
HARDINESS Fully hardy
FLOWERING Summer to autumn

H | *Helianthus annuus* 'Teddy Bear' Sunflower

'TEDDY BEAR' JOINS 'MUSIC BOX' in proving that the beauty of sunflowers isn't necessarily related to height. Young children get more pleasure from growing sunflowers with bright sunny faces at their sort of height, than beanpoles that bob about way above their heads. 'Teddy Bear' is just 90cm (36in) high with a pompon of fuzzy unsunflower-like petals. Sow the seeds in spring where plants are to flower in average, moist but free-draining soil.

OTHER VARIETY 'Sunspot' (large yellow flowerheads).

PLANT PROFILE
HEIGHT 90cm (36in)
SPREAD 60cm (24in)
SITE Full sun
SOIL Neutral to alkaline, average, moist but free-draining
HARDINESS Fully hardy
FLOWERING Summer

Helianthus debilis subsp. *cucumerifolius* Sunflower

SEED COMPANIES KEEP COMING UP with new sunflowers, from record-breaking giants reaching a staggering 8m (25ft) to bushy dwarfs. The multi-branching *H. debilis* subsp. *cucumerifolius* hits a more manageable 1m (3ft), which is a good height for appreciating its beaming, bright and pale yellow (sometimes red-flushed), 15cm (6in) wide flowers. The hairy stems carry an interesting purple mottling. Sow the seeds in spring where plants are to flower in average, moist but free-draining soil.

OTHER VARIETY 'Italian White' (creamy-white to pale primrose-yellow petals and black centres).

PLANT PROFILE
HEIGHT 1m (3ft)
SPREAD 30cm (12in)
SITE Full sun
SOIL Neutral to alkaline, average, moist but free-draining
HARDINESS Fully hardy
FLOWERING Summer to autumn

H | *Heliophila coronopifolia*

THE OVERALL EFFECT OF THIS plant is dainty and gentle, making it useful at the front borders where something subtle and understated is needed. Colours range from pale to bright blue, or even blue-violet, with green–yellow eyes. 'Atlantis' has bright blue flowers with a white eye. Sow the seeds in spring where plants are to flower, but if you want house plants that will flower over winter, sow the seeds in pots in autumn. Grow in fertile, free-draining soil.

OTHER VARIETY *H. leptophylla* (pendent spikes of clear blue flowers).

PLANT PROFILE

HEIGHT 10cm (4in)

SPREAD 30cm (12in)

SITE Full sun

SOIL Fertile, free-draining

HARDINESS Frost hardy

FLOWERING Spring to summer

Heliotropium arborescens 'Marine' Cherry pie

H

THE BEST OF THE CHERRY PIES (also known as heliotrope) offer some of the richest, vanilla-like scents of the summer. All make bushy, short-lived shrubs which can be left as a loose mound or topiarized into a ball on top of a single upright stem. 'Marine' is perfect in a pot as a centrepiece for a garden table, but when growing it in beds create a massed effect to make a show of the colourful flowers. Pot the plants up over winter and keep them in a frost-free place, or sow the seeds each spring under glass, and plant out in fertile, moist but free-draining soil.

OTHER VARIETIES 'Lord Roberts' (compact with light violet-blue flowers); 'White Lady' (compact with white flowers tinged pink in bud).

PLANT PROFILE
HEIGHT 45cm (18in)
SPREAD 45cm (18in)
SITE Full sun
SOIL Fertile, moist but free-draining
HARDINESS Half hardy
FLOWERING Summer

H

Hibiscus acetosella 'Coppertone'

THIS SHORT-LIVED PERENNIAL, grown as an annual in cool climates, has maroon-purple leaves which are up to 30cm (12in) long and resemble the hand-shaped foliage of a maple. Use it in a red colour scheme with dahlias and crocosmias, or as a contrast to bright whites. The funnel-shaped flowers, with their dark purple centres, are approximately 7.5cm (3in) wide. The best choice for flowers is a cultivar of the hardy, shrubby *H. syriacus*, such 'Diana' or 'Woodbridge'. Sow the seeds of 'Coppertone' in spring under glass, and grow in fertile, moist but free-draining soil in a hot, sheltered position.

OTHER VARIETY *H. acetosella* (funnel-shaped, yellow or purple-red flowers, with deep purple centres).

PLANT PROFILE

HEIGHT 90cm (36in)

SPREAD 45cm (18in)

SITE Full sun

SOIL Neutral to alkaline, moist but free-draining

HARDINESS Half hardy

FLOWERING Late summer to autumn

Hibiscus Disco Belle Series Common rose mallow

H

THIS COLOURFUL SERIES OF SMALL ANNUALS is best planted right at the front of the border – unlike large, shrubby *H. syriacus*, which grows head high at the back. Bushy and well covered with 23cm (9in) wide, red, pink or white flowers, they are well worth growing wherever there is a sunny gap between plants. A good alternative is 'Southern Belle', the flowers of which are paler towards the margins. Sow the seeds in spring under glass, and grow outdoors in fertile, moist but free-draining soil.

OTHER VARIETY 'Southern Belle' (dark red flowers, paler towards the margins).

PLANT PROFILE
HEIGHT 50cm (20in)
SPREAD 30cm (12in)
SITE Full sun
SOIL Neutral to alkaline, fertile, moist but free-draining
HARDINESS Min 5°C (41°F)
FLOWERING Summer

H

Hibiscus trionum Flower-of-an-hour

QUICK-GROWING, BEAUTIFUL AND PROLIFIC, *H. trionum* is initially upright before developing lots of flowering branches. The trumpet-shaped flowers have beautifully contrasting creamy-yellow petals and a chocolate-brown centre. The flowers are followed by bladder-like seed capsules. *H. trionum* grows well in containers and is a useful plant for covering the low bare stems of climbers, such as roses. Sow the seeds in spring under glass (soak them first in hot water for an hour) and plant out in neutral to alkaline, fertile, moist but free-draining soil.

OTHER VARIETY *H. cannabinus* (funnel-shaped, pale yellow, occasionally purple-red flowers).

PLANT PROFILE

HEIGHT 75cm (30in)

SPREAD 60cm (24in)

SITE Full sun

SOIL Neutral to alkaline, fertile, moist but free-draining

HARDINESS Half hardy

FLOWERING Summer to early autumn

Hordeum jubatum Squirrel tail grass

H

WITH BARLEY-LIKE, SILKY, SILVERY PLUMES, this small grass often develops a beautiful purple tinge, although towards the end of summer it turns a uniform beige. There are many ways to use this delightful plant in the garden: fill a small bed with it and have strategically placed feature plants rising through its billowing stems, or plant it in swathes as a soft edging for the front of a border. *H. jubatum* is short-lived but self-seeds prolifically. In spring don't be too eager to weed out what appear to be small clumps of lawn grass in the border – you may find it grows into this beauty instead. Sow the seeds in spring or autumn where plants are to grow in average, free-draining soil.

PLANT PROFILE

HEIGHT 50cm (20in)

SPREAD 30cm (12in)

SITE Full sun

SOIL Average, free-draining

HARDINESS Fully hardy

FLOWERING Early and midsummer

H | *Hunnemannia fumariifolia* 'Sunlite' Mexican tulip poppy

NOT ONE OF THE BRIGHT and brash, blood-red perennial poppies, this is a much more delicate and gentle clear yellow. The flowers appear on lax stems among finely dissected, blue-green foliage. It makes a lively contrast with red potentillas or purple salvias. Like most poppies, it hates having its roots disturbed which means the seeds should be sown in spring where plants are to flower. Grow in the garden in average, free-draining soil or in containers to brighten the conservatory in the winter months.

PLANT PROFILE
HEIGHT 60cm (24in)
SPREAD 20cm (8in)
SITE Full sun
SOIL Average, free-draining
HARDINESS Half hardy
FLOWERING Midsummer to late autumn

Iberis amara Candytuft

I

A COTTAGE-GARDEN FAVOURITE since Elizabethan times, candytuft is easy to grow and makes a gentle spread of sweetly scented, white to purplish-white flowers on top of short, stiff, erect stems. It is traditionally grown right at the front of a border with contrasting colours behind. For the biggest flowers go for 'Giant Hyacinth-flowered'. Sow the seeds *in situ* in spring or, for an earlier show of flowers, in autumn. Grow in neutral to alkaline, poor, moist but free-draining soil, and water well in dry spells.

OTHER VARIETY 'Pinnacle' (very fragrant, pure white flowers).

PLANT PROFILE
HEIGHT 45cm (18in)
SPREAD 15cm (6in)
SITE Full sun
SOIL Neutral to alkaline, poor to average, moist but free-draining
HARDINESS Fully hardy
FLOWERING Summer

I *Iberis umbellata* Fairy Series Common candytuft

PRODUCING BUSHY MOUNDS of small, scented flowers, the Fairy Series has cottage garden written all over it, but its short height also makes it a useful filler for gaps between paving and in rock gardens. If you want a candytuft with more vibrant colours, try the Flash Series or other cultivars of *I. umbellata* which offer a range of vibrant pink, purple or carmine-red flowers. Sow the seeds in spring or autumn wherever there is a spare, sunny gap, and from spring on you will enjoy a prolific show of flowers. Grow in poor, moist but free-draining soil that is neutral to alkaline. Water well in dry spells.

OTHER VARIETY 'Iceberg' (pyramids of pure white flowers).

PLANT PROFILE

HEIGHT 30cm (12in)

SPREAD 23cm (9in)

SITE Full sun

SOIL Poor to average, moist but free-draining

HARDINESS Fully hardy

FLOWERING Spring to summer

Impatiens balsamina 'Blackberry Ice' Busy Lizzie

I

IF YOU LIKE YOUR BUSY LIZZIES jazzy strong-coloured and double-flowering, then 'Blackberry Ice' is a good choice. What's more it has white splashed markings on its leaves and purple blooms, and will keep on flowering right through summer. 'Blackberry Ice', like the dwarf 30cm (12in) high, scarlet, pink, violet or white Tom Thumb Series, is a great improvement on the parent *I. balsamina* which, before the plant breeders got to work, was the plant to buy in the 1950s. Sow the seeds in spring on a warm windowsill or in a greenhouse, and plant outdoors in fertile, moist but free-draining soil.

OTHER VARIETY Camellia-flowered Series (large, double, white-mottled, pink or red flowers).

PLANT PROFILE

HEIGHT 70cm (28in)	
SPREAD 45cm (18in)	
SITE Partial shade	
SOIL Fertile, moist but free-draining	
HARDINESS Min 5°C (41°F)	
FLOWERING Summer to early autumn	

Impatiens 'Red Star' Busy Lizzie

UNASHAMEDLY BRIGHT AND BREEZY, the flowers of 'Red Star' look like miniature flags with a white star against a bright red background. The continuous display of flowers is quite astonishing, never letting up the whole summer. At just 15cm (6in) high, the plants need to be grown right at the front of a border or in a pot or windowbox to avoid being swamped by their companions. Sow the seeds in early spring under glass, and grow outdoors in fertile, moist but free-draining soil.

OTHER VARIETY New Guinea Group (lush foliage and brightly coloured flowers).

PLANT PROFILE

HEIGHT 15cm (6in)

SPREAD 15cm (6in)

SITE Partial shade

SOIL Fertile, moist but free-draining

HARDINESS Min 10°C (50°F)

FLOWERING Spring to autumn

Impatiens walleriana Super Elfin Series Busy Lizzie

OF THE MANY EXCELLENT, free-flowering busy Lizzies, this series gets top marks. Short and compact, and in summer covered continuously in blooms, these little gems come in something like 20 different colours. Pastel shades predominate, giving a quiet, soft touch to midsummer schemes. Sow the seeds in early spring under glass, and plant out in fertile, moist but free-draining soil.

OTHER VARIETIES Blitz 2000 Series (taller, multi-branching, dark green foliage, white, orange, pink, red, and violet flowers); Confection Series (double and semi-double flowers in orange, pink, and red).

PLANT PROFILE	
HEIGHT 25cm (10in)	
SPREAD 25cm (10in)	
SITE Partial shade	
SOIL Fertile, moist but free-draining	
HARDINESS Min 10°C (50°F)	
FLOWERING Summer	

I

Ionopsidium acaule Violet cress

OFTEN OVERLOOKED IN GARDENING BOOKS this unusual annual, known as violet cress, produces an abundance of tiny, scented, cross-shaped flowers all summer, above low clumps of mid-green leaves. It is an extremely useful plant for filling gaps between paving and dotting around in the rock garden. An easy-to-grow annual, simply scatter seeds in spring where plants are to flower, in average, moist but free-draining soil.

PLANT PROFILE
HEIGHT 8cm (3in)
SPREAD 2.5cm (1in)
SITE Partial shade
SOIL Moist but free-draining
HARDINESS Half hardy
FLOWERING Summer

Ipomoea coccinea Red morning glory

I

WHEREVER THERE IS A GAP FOR A CLIMBER up a wall or over a shrub, try this scarlet-flowering, yellow-throated ipomoea. It twines up and around support structures (horizontal wires or stems), and gives a much-needed dash of zesty colour. Sow the pre-soaked seeds in spring under glass, and grow outdoors in average, free-draining soil. Provide shelter from cold, drying winds, and a sturdy support structure, such as adjacent shrubs or a small frame. The seeds are toxic if ingested.

OTHER VARIETY *I. tricolor* (funnel-shaped, bright sky-blue to purple flowers with white tubes, golden yellow inside at the bases).

PLANT PROFILE
HEIGHT 4m (12ft)
SITE Full sun
SOIL Average, free-draining
HARDINESS Min 7°C (45°F)
FLOWERING Summer

I

Ipomoea lobata Spanish flag

NOVICE GARDENERS OFTEN BEGIN BY GROWING the showy ipomoeas known as morning glories with their brightly coloured, trumpet-like flowers, and then they turn to this – a more modest and intriguing variety. The twisting, twining, climbing stems of Spanish flag have a red tinge, and the small flowers are slightly curved and tubular. Initially scarlet, they gradually fade to orange, yellow and then white. Sow the seed in spring under glass, and plant out in average, free-draining soil. As with all ipomoeas, provide shelter from cold, drying winds, and a good support structure. The seed is toxic if ingested.

OTHER VARIETY *I. nil* 'Chocolate' (red-chocolate-brown flowers).

PLANT PROFILE	
HEIGHT 5m (15ft)	
SITE Full sun	
SOIL Average, free-draining	
HARDINESS Min 10°C (50°F)	
FLOWERING Summer to autumn	

Ipomoea quamoclit Star glory

I

ONE OF THE VERY BEST annual climbers, *I. quamoclit* has fine, fern-like leaves and small, funnel-shaped, bright red (sometimes white) flowers. Provide support for its twining growth, whether it be a wigwam of canes wrapped round with string or wire, or adjacent shrubs and climbers for it to climb through. Sow the pre-soaked seeds in spring under glass, and plant out in average, free-draining soil, providing shelter from cold, drying winds. The seed is toxic.

HEIGHT 2m (6ft)

SITE Full sun

SOIL Average, free-draining

HARDINESS Min 7°C (45°F)

FLOWERING Summer

OTHER VARIETY *I. nil* 'Scarlett O'Hara' (bright red flowers).

Ipomoea tricolor 'Heavenly Blue' Morning glory

THE BEST-KNOWN MORNING GLORY, 'Heavenly Blue' is a quick-sprinting, twining climber with beautiful, blue, funnel-shaped flowers. Wherever there is a suitable climbing frame in the garden – from the bare stems of a climbing rose to a non-flowering shrub – send a morning glory to scramble over it. *I. tricolor* 'Grandpa Otts' has sensational violet-blue petals with ruby-red centres. Sow the seeds (which are toxic if ingested) in spring under glass, and plant outdoors in average, free-draining soil. Provide shelter from cold, drying winds.

OTHER VARIETY 'Flying Saucers' (variably marbled, white and purple-blue flowers).

PLANT PROFILE
HEIGHT 4m (12ft)
SITE Full sun
SOIL Average, free-draining
HARDINESS Min 7°C (45°F)
FLOWERING Summer

Ipomopsis aggregata Skyrocket

I

A RATHER IMPRESSIVE RED-FLOWERING annual or biennial, skyrocket, which is also known as scarlet gilia, combines colourful, tubular flowers on upright, branching stems with finely divided leaves. You can sow the seeds either in late winter or early spring under glass to flower in summer. Alternatively, for a slightly earlier show, sow the seeds in summer and overwinter the plants in a cold frame. Plant out in fertile, free-draining soil.

PLANT PROFILE

HEIGHT 1m (3ft)

SPREAD 30cm (12in)

SITE Sun

SOIL Fertile, free-draining

HARDINESS Half hardy

FLOWERING Midsummer to early autumn

I *Isatis tinctoria* Woad

PERFECT FOR AN OLD-FASHIONED COTTAGE GARDEN, the leaves of this plant were once used to make blue dye. A short-lived perennial, woad is usually grown as a biennial. Once established, the plant self-seeds freely. The grey-green leaves are 10cm (4in) long and appear below tall stems which are topped by loose clusters of bright yellow flowers. The flowers are followed by attractive seed pods. Sow the seeds in autumn in a cold frame and plant out in fairly rich, moist but free-draining soil.

PLANT PROFILE

HEIGHT 1.2m (4ft)

SPREAD 45cm (18in)

SITE Full sun

SOIL Average, moist but free-draining

HARDINESS Fully hardy

FLOWERING Early summer

Jamesbrittenia SUMATRA INDIGO ('Yagemon')

THE FIVE-PETALLED FLOWERS of this beautiful plant appear in great profusion over a long period, starting in late spring. The bushy, mound-forming, semi-trailing stems and serrated leaves are accompanied by a great mass of yellow-eyed, purple-indigo flowers, making it a beautiful plant for hanging baskets. It will also grow well at the front of a border or in a rock or gravel garden. Propagate from summer cuttings, and grow in fertile, free-draining soil.

PLANT PROFILE
HEIGHT 30cm (12in)
SPREAD 30cm (12in)
SITE Sun or partial shade
SOIL Fertile, free-draining
HARDINESS Min 5°C (41°F)
FLOWERING Late spring and summer

L | *Lablab purpureus* Egyptian bean

ORIGINALLY FROM TROPICAL AFRICA, the Egyptian bean is much too tender to survive outside in winter in north-west Europe, and is best grown as an annual. The twining stems put on a rampant mass of growth (provide a very strong support structure), and with its scented, pea-like flowers, it's a bit like a high-powered runner bean. The 10–15cm (4–6in) long green pods, often flushed purple, and the white to red-brown, brown or black beans are edible after soaking. Sow the seeds in spring under glass, and grow outdoors in any free-draining soil. For the best crop of beans, apply a liquid fertilizer every 10 to 14 days in early summer until flowering.

PLANT PROFILE

HEIGHT 6m (20ft)

SITE Full sun

SOIL Free-draining

HARDINESS Min 7°C (45°F)

FLOWERING Summer and autumn

Lagurus ovatus Hare's tail

L

YOU WILL FIND CLUMPS of this pretty annual grass growing in the wild on sandy Mediterranean sites near the sea. The soft, tactile leaves appear first, followed by the hairy flowerheads which look like short, stumpy hares' or rabbits' tails. These start off pale green before turning beige. Fresh or dried, they look good in flower arrangements, and should be picked before they fully mature. Sow the seeds *in situ* in spring, or sow in a cold frame in autumn. Grow in very light, sandy, free-draining soil.

PLANT PROFILE	
HEIGHT 50cm (20in)	
SPREAD 30cm (12in)	
SITE Full sun	
SOIL Light, sandy, free-draining	
HARDINESS Fully hardy	
FLOWERING Summer	

L

Lamarckia aurea Golden top

A BEAUTIFUL AND UNUSUAL SMALL GRASS, golden top makes a tuft of pale green leaves. The flowers at the top of the stems are like little silvery bristles that point down at 45 degree angles. They start off golden yellow or white-green, then turn silver, and often end up with a purple tinge. They are highly valued in fresh and dried-flower arrangements. Sow the seeds from early to late spring in batches where plants are to grow in light, sandy, free-draining soil. You can also sow the seeds in late spring in pots in a cold frame, using them to replace the first batch when they fade in midsummer.

PLANT PROFILE

HEIGHT 30cm (12in)

SPREAD 25cm (10in)

SITE Full sun

SOIL Light, sandy, free-draining

HARDINESS Fully hardy

FLOWERING Mid-spring to summer

PLANT SUPPORT

A cane wigwam, bound with string, allows air to circulate through plants which helps prevent mildew lets wind waft the scent around the garden.

Lathyrus odoratus Sweet pea

L

THE BEST SWEET PEAS have a far-reaching, extraordinary scent and are exquisitely coloured. The plants climb with twining tendrils and need a tall cane wigwam for support (*see inset*); when young, it's a good idea to start training them up twiggy sticks. Sow the seeds (soaking them first) in pots in a cold frame in autumn or early spring. When the seedlings reach 8cm (3in) tall, pinch out the growing tips to encourage bushiness. Plant out after the last frost in fertile, free-draining soil. Feed every two weeks over summer with a liquid fertilizer.

OTHER VARIETY Continental Group (red, blue, pink or white flowers).

PLANT PROFILE

HEIGHT 2m (6ft)

SITE Full sun or partial shade

SOIL Fertile, free-draining

HARDINESS Fully hardy

FLOWERING Summer to early autumn

L | *Lathyrus odoratus* Bijou Group Sweet pea

NOT ALL SWEET PEAS ARE VIGOROUS CLIMBERS – the slightly scented Bijou Group makes a lovely mini show for the front of a colourful cottage-garden border. A few short twigs is all the support they need. As with all sweet peas, the more you keep cutting the flowers for flower arrangements, the more new buds keep appearing. They come in pretty shades of pink, blue, red, and white. Soak and then sow the seeds in pots in a cold frame in autumn or early spring. When the young plants reach 8cm (3in) tall, pinch out the growing tips to encourage bushiness. Plant out after the last frost in fertile, free-draining soil. Provide a liquid feed every two weeks in summer.

OTHER VARIETY 'Pink Cupid' (strong scent, pink and white flowers).

PLANT PROFILE

HEIGHT 45cm (18in)

SPREAD 45cm (18in)

SITE Full sun or partial shade

SOIL Fertile, free-draining

HARDINESS Fully hardy

FLOWERING Summer to early autumn

Lathyrus sativus Chickling pea

THIS MEMBER OF THE SWEET PEA FAMILY is grown as a crop for animal feed, but it has lots of virtues as a border plant. The dainty flowers are initially blue and gradually fade to white, sometimes with pink veins. Regular deadheading will encourage flower production. The stems are also quite a feature, being strangely angular and winged. Soak and then sow the seeds in pots in a cold frame in autumn or early spring. When the plants reach 8cm (3in) tall, pinch out the tips to encourage bushiness. Plant out after the last frost in fertile, free-draining soil. Give a liquid feed every fortnight in summer.

OTHER VARIETY *L. odoratus* Explorer Group (mid-blue, navy blue, crimson, scarlet, rose-pink, light pink, purple or white wavy flowers).

PLANT PROFILE
HEIGHT 1m (3ft)
SPREAD 45cm (18in)
SITE Full sun or partial shade
SOIL Fertile, free-draining
HARDINESS Fully hardy
FLOWERING Summer

L

Lavatera trimestris 'Silver Cup' Mallow

THE TRIMESTRIS ANNUAL MALLOWS are a big hit in cottage gardens, and 'Silver Cup' is one of the best. Multi-branching, multi-flowering and sturdy, it puts on a lavish show of 12cm (5in) wide sugar-pink blooms with dark veins. Individual flowers do not last long but new replacements keep appearing. Other good choices include white-flowered 'Mont Blanc' and 'Ruby Regis', which is a delicate pink with a dark eye and purple veins. Sow the seeds in mid- to late spring where plants are to flower, in average, light, free-draining soil.

OTHER VARIETY 'Loveliness' (deep rose-pink flowers).

PLANT PROFILE

HEIGHT 75cm (30in)

SPREAD 45cm (18in)

SITE Full sun

SOIL Average, free-draining

HARDINESS Fully hardy

FLOWERING Summer

Layia platyglossa Tidy tips

L

WHAT MARKS OUT THIS CALIFORNIAN ANNUAL is the long summer show of white-tipped, yellow flowers, each with a deep golden yellow eye, backed by softly hairy, grey-green leaves. Since it likes poor to average, light, sandy soil, it is ideal for a Mediterranean-type, hot, dry garden or border. Do not make the mistake of trying to grow it in rich soil because the stems will become lax and soft. Sow the seeds in early spring or autumn where plants are to flower. The blooms are exceptionally good for cutting.

PLANT PROFILE
HEIGHT 45cm (18in)
SPREAD 30cm (12in)
SITE Full sun
SOIL Poor, free-draining
HARDINESS Fully hardy
FLOWERING Summer to autumn

L

Legousia speculum-veneris Venus's looking glass

A COLOURFUL, BUSHY ANNUAL for wildflower or Mediterranean-type gardens, *L. speculum-veneris* has saucer-shaped, violet-blue (sometimes white or pale purple) flowers with a white centre. The flowers, measuring 2.5cm (1in) wide, are quite unusual and perk up cut-flower displays. Sow the seeds in autumn or mid-spring where plants are to flower. The plant is often found growing wild in stony ground in southern Europe, from Spain to Greece, and further east in Iraq and Iran; it is, therefore, happiest in light, free-draining soil.

PLANT PROFILE

HEIGHT 30cm (12in)

SPREAD 10cm (4in)

SITE Full sun or partial shade

SOIL Poor, free-draining

HARDINESS Fully hardy

FLOWERING Early summer to autumn

Leucanthemum paludosum

L

SHORT, BUSHY AND HAIRY, *L. paludosum* has two main features: the solitary white flowers with yellow disc-like eyes; and the different shaped leaves – spoon-shaped ones at the base of the stem, and wedge-shaped ones further up. 'Show Star' is more eye-catching than its parent plant, *L. paludosum*, and has a spread of bright yellow flowers and wavy-edged leaves. Don't confuse either with *L.* x *superbum* (shasta daisy), which is completely different. Sow the seeds *in situ* in spring in average, moist but free-draining soil.

OTHER VARIETY *L. atratum* (yellow-centred white flowers).

PLANT PROFILE
HEIGHT 15cm (6in)
SPREAD 20cm (8in)
SITE Full sun or partial shade
SOIL Average, moist but free-draining
HARDINESS Fully hardy
FLOWERING Summer

L | *Limnanthes douglasii* Poached egg plant

PERHAPS THE COMMON NAME rather overdoes the poetic licence, but the flowers do have a yolk-yellow centre surrounded by a distinctive white outer ring. The flowers, which start opening at grass level in late spring, are very attractive to bees and hoverflies. Once established, the plant will self-seed freely to form spreading sheets, and is best grown where it can run unrestricted, for example, in large gaps between paving. If you are willing to weed out unwanted seedlings, you can easily keep it within bounds; in which case it makes a jolly plant for the rock garden. Sow the seeds in spring or autumn where plants are to flower in fertile, moist but free-draining soil.

PLANT PROFILE

HEIGHT 15cm (6in)

SPREAD 15cm (6in) or more

SITE Full sun

SOIL Fertile, moist but free-draining

HARDINESS Fully hardy

FLOWERING Late spring to autumn

DRYING FLOWERS

The pretty flowers of sea lavender look great in dried arrangements. Cut the flowers and hang them upside down in a cool, dry, dark place.

Limonium sinuatum Fortress Series Sea lavender

L

THE VIVID COLOURS OF THE FORTRESS SERIES score high points in the garden and in fresh or dried flower displays – in fact, this series is just about the best sea lavender for cut flowers. They are small and funnel-shaped, opening in clusters on strong, multi-branching stems, and give a horizontal spread of blooms. Other good forms include California Series with its strong colours, and the Sunburst Series (also good for cutting) in warm shades, including orange-peach and rose-red. Sow the seeds in early spring under glass, and plant out in sandy, free-draining soil.

OTHER VARIETY Petite Bouquet Series (dwarf, with tightly bunched spikelets in a variety of colours).

PLANT PROFILE	
HEIGHT 60cm (24in)	
SPREAD 30cm (12in)	
SITE Full sun	
SOIL Free-draining	
HARDINESS Frost hardy	
FLOWERING Summer and early autumn	

L

Linanthus grandiflorus Mountain phlox

SHORTER THAN THE TRADITIONAL BORDER PHLOX, this Californian annual has dense heads of small open flowers which make very good cut flowers. Mountain phlox is typically grown in wildflower gardens or to the front of beds and borders. It can also be grown as a conservatory pot plant. Even smaller phlox include *L. dianthiflorus* (ground pink), from 5–12cm (2–5in) high, and *L. nuttallii* which measures about 15cm (6in). Sow the seeds in spring where plants are to flower, and grow in light, free-draining soil.

OTHER VARIETY *L. dianthiflorus* (yellow-throated, white, pink or lilac-blue flowers).

PLANT PROFILE
HEIGHT 50cm (20in)
SPREAD 23cm (9in)
SITE Full sun
SOIL Light, free-draining
HARDINESS Fully hardy
FLOWERING Spring to summer

Linaria maroccana 'Northern Lights' Toadflax

POPULAR, SLENDER AND GOOD FOR CUT FLOWERS, 'Northern Lights' offers long-lasting blooms in a wide range of colours. Plants are excellent in cottage gardens, forming swirls and sweeps of yellow, rose-pink, lavender, white, carmine, orange and salmon-pink around shrubs. Because they need light, sandy, free-draining soil, they also add plenty of life to Mediterranean-style gardens. Sow the seeds in spring where plants are to flower. Once they have flowered, the plants will readily self-seed.

OTHER VARIETIES 'Fairy Bouquet' (yellow, rose-pink, salmon-pink, orange, carmine, lavender, and white); 'Ruby King' (wine-red flowers); 'White Pearl' (pure white flowers).

PLANT PROFILE	
HEIGHT 60cm (24in)	
SPREAD 15cm (6in)	
SITE Full sun	
SOIL Average, free-draining	
HARDINESS Fully hardy	
FLOWERING Summer	

L *Linaria reticulata* 'Crown Jewels' **Purple–net toadflax**

THE HIGHLY DISTINCTIVE, TWO-LIPPED flowers of 'Crown Jewels' are best arranged in groups for maximum impact. The flower colours are rich and vibrant (orange, red, maroon-red, and golden yellow) while the narrow leaves are in a more subdued shade of blue-green. Sow the seeds in spring where plants are to flower, in light, average (sandy if possible), free-draining soil. Once they have bloomed, the plants will self-seed giving extra flowers the following year.

OTHER VARIETY *L. maroccana* (violet-purple, occasionally pink or white flowers).

PLANT PROFILE

HEIGHT 23cm (9in)

SPREAD 23cm (9in)

SITE Full sun

SOIL Average, free-draining

HARDINESS Fully hardy

FLOWERING Late spring and summer

Lindheimera texana Star daisy

L

A BEAUTIFUL, UPRIGHT, DAISY-LIKE ANNUAL from Texas, *L. texana* has small flowers, about 2.5cm (1in) wide, in golden yellow to creamy-yellow with a tiny green-yellow eye. The plants make a lovely informal show in wildflower gardens or in large containers. Sow the seeds in spring where plants are to flower. In its native habitat it is found growing in dry, limestone prairies; in the garden give it average soil that is light and free-draining.

PLANT PROFILE

HEIGHT 60cm (24in)

SPREAD 30cm (12in)

SITE Full sun

SOIL Average, free-draining

HARDINESS Fully hardy

FLOWERING Late spring and summer

L

Linum grandiflorum 'Rubrum' Flowering flax

THE FIVE-PETALLED, SAUCER-SHAPED FLOWERS of 'Rubrum' may not last long, but others quickly open to take their place, giving a long flowering period. The plant makes an excellent filler in borders wherever there is a smallish gap. Other reds are available but 'Rubrum' is certainly the best of the bunch, with dazzling crimson petals surrounding an intense dark red centre. Mix it with one of the white forms, in particular 'Bright Eyes,' which is the same height as 'Rubrum' with ivory-white petals and a brownish-red eye. Sow the seeds from late summer to autumn or in spring where plants are to flower, in light, free-draining soil.

PLANT PROFILE

HEIGHT 45cm (18in)

SPREAD 15cm (6in)

SITE Full sun

SOIL Average, free-draining

HARDINESS Fully hardy

FLOWERING Summer and autumn

Linum usitatissimum Common flax

L

THIS FLAX IS COMMERCIALLY GROWN to make linen and linseed oil, but in the garden it is simply enjoyed for its beautiful, saucer-shaped, sky-blue flowers. Planted in a border, they add a lovely soft hue to pastel schemes. The flowers are followed by straw-coloured, rounded capsules. Sow the seeds from late summer to autumn, or in the spring, where plants are to flower, and grow in average, light, free-draining soil.

PLANT PROFILE
HEIGHT 90cm (36in)
SPREAD 20cm (8in)
SITE Full sun
SOIL Average, free-draining
HARDINESS Fully hardy
FLOWERING Summer

OTHER VARIETY *L. grandiflorum* 'Caeruleum' (purple-blue flowers).

L | *Lobelia erinus* Cascade Series

ANNUAL LOBELIAS ARE TRADITIONALLY GROWN either in beds, when they are of the compact, bushy kind, or in hanging baskets when they are sprawling and trailing. The Cascade Series is a trailing type and forms an erupting, tangled mass of flowering stems in a wide range of colours, from blue to red, lilac and white. They can also be grown to tumble over the sides of windowboxes, or spread across the soil. Alternatively, try the new, trailing, long-flowering Regatta Series which offers lovely blue and white bicolour blooms. Sow the seed in late winter under glass, or late summer for spring flowering, and plant out in moist, fertile soil. Lobelia is toxic if ingested.

OTHER VARIETY 'Sapphire' (trailing with blue, white-eyed flowers).

PLANT PROFILE
HEIGHT 15cm (6in)
SPREAD 15cm (6in)
SITE Full sun or partial shade
SOIL Moist, fertile
HARDINESS Half hardy
FLOWERING Summer to autumn

Lobelia erinus 'Snowball'

L

THE PRETTY, SNOW-WHITE FLOWERS of this bushy cultivar are occasionally interspersed with pale blue blooms. Use 'Snowball' on its own along the edges of garden paths, or contrast its flowers with the deep blue tones of 'Crystal Palace'. It also looks great in containers and windowboxes. Sow the seeds from late winter to mid-spring under glass (germination usually takes between 14 and 21 days), and grow plants in moist soil in a sunny spot. As with all lobelias, 'Snowball' is harmful if eaten, and is best avoided in garden schemes where young children play.

OTHER VARIETIES 'Cobalt Blue' (intense mid-blue flowers); Riviera Series (lilac-blue, sky-blue or mottled blue flowers).

PLANT PROFILE
HEIGHT 15cm (6in)
SPREAD 15cm (6in)
SITE Full sun or partial shade
SOIL Moist, fertile
HARDINESS Half hardy
FLOWERING Summer

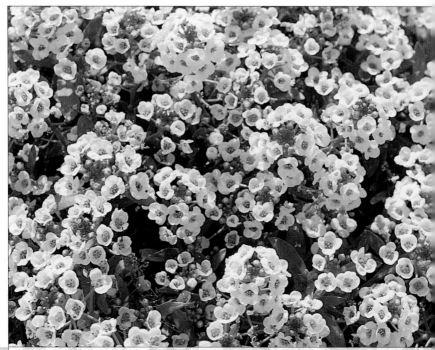

L

Lobularia maritima 'Snow Crystals' Sweet Alison

AN ALL-TIME FAVOURITE ANNUAL, sweet Alison was originally white but is now available in a range of colours, including purple, pink, and apricot. 'Snow Crystals' produces small mounds of white flowers, and is perfect for planting between red roses and for filling gaps beside paths, in crazy paving and to the front of a border. For a multicoloured look, grow 'Snow Crystals' together with the likes of the Easter Bonnet Series, with its reddish-purple blooms, and 'New Purple'. Sow the seeds in late spring in pots or where plants are to flower, and grow in light, free-draining soil.

OTHER VARIETIES 'Navy Blue' (very compact, with deep purple flowers); 'Wonderland Rose' (rose-pink flowers).

PLANT PROFILE	
HEIGHT	25cm (10in)
SPREAD	25cm (10in)
SITE	Full sun
SOIL	Average, free-draining
HARDINESS	Fully hardy
FLOWERING	Summer

PAPERY SEEDHEADS

Leave the papery, semi-translucent seedheads of honesty in place for late summer and autumn interest, or cut them for dried arrangements.

Lunaria annua 'Variegata' Honesty

L

AN INDISPENSABLE COTTAGE-GARDEN ANNUAL, honesty self-seeds prolifically around the garden. It produces an extremely useful, tallish plant for the spring garden and 'Variegata', with its free-and-easy, open, airy look and green and white leaves, makes an effective pairing with clumps of daffodils. The seed pods are paper thin and a boon to dried-flower arrangements; remove the pods as their green colour fades and hang in a cool, dry, airy place. Sow the seeds in early summer where plants are to flower, and grow in fertile, moist but free-draining soil.

OTHER VARIETIES *L. annua* var. *albiflora* (white flowers); 'Munstead Purple' (deep red-purple flowers).

PLANT PROFILE
HEIGHT 90cm (36in)
SPREAD 30cm (12in)
SITE Full sun or partial
SOIL Fertile, moist but free-draining
HARDINESS Fully hardy
FLOWERING Late spring and summer

L | *Lupinus nanus* 'Pixie Delight' Lupin

'PIXIE DELIGHT' IS ON THE SHORT AND BUSHY SIDE compared with other traditional lupins which are around 90cm (36in) tall. This shorter cultivar comes in a range of attractive colours, many with bicoloured flowers. Plants can be grown alone in gaps in the border or packed together in highly impressive clumps. The leaves are like opened hands, with the fingers angled outwards and upwards. Sow the seeds (pre-soaked for 24 hours) in spring or autumn in pots, and grow in slightly acid, light, free-draining soil.

OTHER VARIETY *L. luteus* 'Yellow Javelin' (pea-like, bright golden yellow flowers).

PLANT PROFILE

HEIGHT 50cm (20in)

SPREAD 23cm (9in)

SITE Full sun or partial shade

SOIL Slightly acid, average, free-draining

HARDINESS Fully hardy

FLOWERING Summer

Lupinus texensis Texas bluebonnet

L

THE WELL-KNOWN, COTTAGE GARDEN LUPINS have vertical, candle-like arrangements of flowers, up to 60cm (24in) long, that seem to launch themselves out of the foliage. *L. texensis* is slightly different because the whole plant is more spreading and bushy, and the flower spikes are shorter – about 8cm (3in) long – and more closely packed together. Both kinds share the same distinctive leaves which resemble open hands. Sow the seeds (pre-soaked for 24 hours) in pots in spring or autumn. Grow in slightly acid, light, free-draining soil.

OTHER VARIETY *L. mutabilis* (pea-like flowers, with pale purple-blue petals, yellow standard petals and deep-blue wing petals).

PLANT PROFILE
HEIGHT 30cm (12in)
SPREAD 23cm (9in)
SITE Full sun or partial shade
SOIL Slightly acid, average, free-draining
HARDINESS Fully hardy
FLOWERING Summer

M | *Malcolmia maritima* Virginian stock

WORTH GROWING IN GRAVEL GARDENS, seaside gardens or in gaps in paving, this Mediterranean annual makes a pretty show of four-petalled flowers. The blooms keep going right through summer, and a small bunch picked for a posy offers a gentle, sweet scent. You only need to grow a few plants initially because they self-seed freely and will quickly create scattered clumps. Sow the seeds from late spring where plants are to flower, and provide average, free-draining soil with, if possible, some shade from the midday sun.

OTHER VARIETY Compacta Series (white, pink, red or purple flowers).

PLANT PROFILE
HEIGHT 40cm (16in)
SPREAD 15cm (6in)
SITE Full sun
SOIL Average, free-draining
HARDINESS Fully hardy
FLOWERING Spring to autumn

Malope trifida **Annual mallow**

M

A BIT LIKE A SHORT, BUSHY HOLLYHOCK, the annual mallow is a highly useful plant in cottage gardens. It is just the right height for the middle of the border and, at just 23cm (9in) wide, squeezes into small gaps. The flowers and leaves are big enough to make an impact, the former being 5–8cm (2–3in) wide, and the latter up to 10cm (4in) long. Sow the seeds in early spring under glass, or in mid-spring where plants are to flower, in average, moist but free-draining soil.

OTHER VARIETIES 'Rosea'(rose-red flowers); 'Vulcan' (bright magenta-pink flowers); 'White Queen' (pure white flowers).

PLANT PROFILE
HEIGHT 90cm (36in)
SPREAD 23cm (9in)
SITE Full sun
SOIL Average, moist but free-draining
HARDINESS Fully hardy
FLOWERING Summer to autumn

M | *Matricaria recutita* Mayweed

ALSO KNOWN AS GERMAN CAMOMILE, but less scented than
Chamaemelum nobile (lawn camomile), the flowers of *M. recutita* are
said to be a sedative, reduce inflammation, cure bad hair days and
tackle travel sickness, but try it at your own risk. What is certain is
that the tiny, daisy-like flowers and the finely dissected leaves make
a lovely cottage-garden or wildflower show. Sow the seeds in mid-
spring where plants are to flower, in average, free-draining soil. Once
established it will self-seed freely and ensure a supply of new plants.

PLANT PROFILE

HEIGHT 50cm (20in)

SPREAD 30cm (12in)

SITE Full sun

SOIL Average, free-draining

HARDINESS Fully hardy

FLOWERING Late spring
to late summer

Matthiola incana Cinderella Series Stock

M

THERE ARE MANY COLOURFUL, sweet, clove-scented cultivars of *M. incana*, but the Cinderella Series deserves its place right at the top of the list. The short plants have highly attractive, eye-catching double flowers, and are just right for the front of a cottage garden border where they will stand smartly upright. Sow the seeds of the Cinderella Series in early spring under glass, and grow in a sheltered site in average, moist but free-draining, neutral to slightly alkaline soil.

OTHER VARIETIES Legacy Series (scarlet-red, crimson-red, rose-pink, lavender-blue, white, and creamy-yellow flowers); Midget Series (flowers in a range of pastel and deeper tones).

PLANT PROFILE

HEIGHT 25cm (10in)

SPREAD 25cm (10in)

SITE Full sun

SOIL Neutral to slightly alkaline, average, moist but free-draining,

HARDINESS Fully hardy

FLOWERING Late spring to summer

M | *Matthiola longipetala* subsp. *bicornis* Night–scented stock

AN ABSOLUTELY INDISPENSABLE ANNUAL, night-scented stock is a small, not too fantastically showy plant that releases a sweet, heady perfume in the evenings. Plant it underneath windows in boxes, and in pots wherever you sit out in the garden in the early evening. The one big problem is slugs – given a chance they will chomp through the young stems the moment they appear. Sow the seeds in succession from spring where plants are to flower, in a sheltered site on average, moist but free-draining, neutral to alkaline soil.

OTHER VARIETY *M. incana* (sweet-scented, mauve, purple, violet, pink or white flowers).

PLANT PROFILE

HEIGHT 35cm (14in)

SPREAD 23cm (9in)

SITE Full sun

SOIL Neutral to slightly alkaline, average, moist but free-draining

HARDINESS Fully hardy

FLOWERING Summer

Maurandya barclayana

M

THE CLIMBING, TWINING, VIGOROUS STEMS of *M. barclayana* shoot up very quickly in summer, producing masses of foxglove-like tubular flowers, usually with white throats. It is far too tender to survive winters in north-west Europe, but can easily be grown from seed in the spring. It produces plenty of leafy growth and gives a colourful show trained up a pergola, over an old shed or supported on horizontal wires fixed to a warm wall. A good alternative is the nearly identical *Lophospermum scandens*. Sow the seeds in spring under glass, and plant out in average, moist but free-draining soil.

PLANT PROFILE

HEIGHT 5m (15ft)

SITE Full sun

SOIL Average, moist but free-draining

HARDINESS Half hardy

FLOWERING Summer to autumn

M | *Mentzelia lindleyi* Blazing star

BLAZING IS A HIGHLY APPROPRIATE WORD to describe this plant, because when the small, golden-yellow flowers open in early summer they put on a really flashy show. You can encourage a second flush of flowers by shearing over the plant when the first lot has faded – leave 5cm (2in) of stem above ground. This will force up new, vigorous growth. The flowers look particularly attractive set against the web of narrow, grey-green leaves. Grow blazing star near a door or under a window because in the evening it releases a delicious scent. Sow the seeds in spring where plants are to flower, in average, free-draining soil in a sheltered site. Water plants well for good results.

PLANT PROFILE

HEIGHT 70cm (28in)

SPREAD 23cm (9in)

SITE Full sun

SOIL Average, free-draining

HARDINESS Fully hardy

FLOWERING Summer

Mimosa pudica Humble plant

THIS IS THE FAMOUS TOUCH–THE–LEAVES–AND–WATCH PLANT – lightly brush the fronds and they quickly respond by closing up like splayed fingers coming together. It takes about an hour for the leaves to unclasp. The leaves also tend to close at night and open in the morning. An exotic from tropical America, people are surprised to learn that *M. pudica* is easy to grow as an annual for a warm conservatory. Sow the seeds on a sunny windowsill at 18°C (64°F) in pots set on a bed of gravel in a plastic tray. Keep the tray topped up with warm water to the level of the gravel because the plant needs a high level of humidity. It is also very tender and will not survive cold nights outside.

PLANT PROFILE
HEIGHT 75cm (30in)
SPREAD 90cm (36in)
SITE Full sun
SOIL Average, free-draining
HARDINESS Min 13°C (55°F)
FLOWERING Summer

M | *Mimulus* 'Malibu' Monkey flower

IF YOU LIKE FLASHY, COLOURFUL ANNUALS as gap fillers or showy blocks of colour, you should start growing the monkey flower. All varieties have intriguing two-lipped flowers and come in a rich range of colours (many are bicoloured). They are happy in damp soil and in shade (most annuals demand full sun), and some forms flower within eight weeks of sowing. 'Malibu' is short and compact, and can be grown to the front of a bed or in containers. Sow the seeds in spring under glass, and provide fertile, damp soil.

OTHER VARIETY 'Calypso' (self-coloured, bicoloured, and spotted flowers in a wide colour range).

PLANT PROFILE

HEIGHT 15cm (6in)

SPREAD 15cm (6in)

SITE Full sun or light dappled shade

SOIL Fertile, damp

HARDINESS Fully hardy

FLOWERING Summer

Mirabilis jalapa Four o'clock flower

M

THE INTRIGUING FOUR O'CLOCK FLOWER has three main features. First, it keeps its flowers closed until late afternoon on sunny days (when overcast, they are open all day), and by the time the sun rises the next morning they will have closed again. Second, it has the scent of a fresh-cut lemon. And third, at any one time a plant can have different coloured flowers (red, pink, magenta, yellow or white), some of which are striped. No wonder its other common name is the marvel of Peru. Sow the seeds in early spring, or buy a bulb-like tuber, and plant in average, free-draining soil. Water it well during the growing season. In autumn before the first frost, dig up the tubers and store them in pots over the winter in a frost-free greenhouse.

PLANT PROFILE	
HEIGHT	60cm (24in)
SPREAD	60cm (24in)
SITE	Full sun
SOIL	Average, free-draining
HARDINESS	Frost hardy
FLOWERING	Summer

M | *Moluccella laevis* Bells of Ireland

QUIRKY YET ELEGANT, BELLS OF IRELAND are perfect for a cottage garden. Their erect spires are crowded with deeply scalloped leaves and, in late summer, pale green calyxes (leaf-like forms at the base of the flower that protect the bud) surround and cup the tiny flowers deep inside. Lovely in flower arrangements, but watch your fingers on the five sharp thorns near the bells. Growing the seeds is notoriously tricky, but the best tip is to chill them in the fridge for five days then soak them overnight in tepid water before sowing. The seeds need light to germinate, and should be sprinkled on the surface of the compost without a covering of soil. Have patience because they are quite slow to take off. Plant outdoors in average, moist but free-draining soil.

PLANT PROFILE

HEIGHT 90cm (36in)

SPREAD 23cm (9in)

SITE Full sun

SOIL Average, moist but free-draining

HARDINESS Half hardy

FLOWERING Late summer

Monopsis MIDNIGHT ('Yagemon')

M

A GOOD CHOICE FOR HANGING BASKETS, with a profusion of trailing stems covered in flowers that keep blooming for a long period in bright sun or light shade. This plant can also be grown in pots, to the front of a border or to edge a path where its ground-hugging growth and dense foliage will soften the hard paving. Propagate from summer cuttings, and grow in fertile, free-draining soil.

PLANT PROFILE

HEIGHT 15cm (6in)

SPREAD 45cm (18in)

SITE Sun or light shade

SOIL Fertile, free-draining

HARDINESS Min 5°C (41°F)

FLOWERING Summer

M | *Myosotis sylvatica* 'Music' Forget–me–not

SHORT, SELF-SEEDING AND EASY TO GROW, forget-me-nots are the
quintessential spring plants ideal for creating a carpet of colour.
The flowers offer the chance for smart combinations, two of the
very best being forget-me-nots among bright yellow 'West Point'
tulips, and plantings of daffodils. They can also be used wherever
there is a gap at the front of a border. 'Music' scores over many
forget-me-nots by being on the tall side; most plants are about 15cm
(6in) high. Sow the seeds in early summer in pots in a cold frame,
and grow in average to poor, moist but well-drained soil.

OTHER VARIETIES 'Blue Ball' (azure flowers); 'Pompadour' (compact
and ball-shaped, with large, deep rose-pink flowers).

PLANT PROFILE

HEIGHT 25cm (10in)

SPREAD 15cm (6in)

SITE Full sun or partial
shade

SOIL Average to poor,
moist but free-draining

HARDINESS Fully hardy

FLOWERING Spring to
early summer

Nemesia strumosa 'Prince of Orange'

N

ARCHETYPAL COTTAGE-GARDEN PLANTS, the two-lipped South African nemesias will fill the garden with their bright colours during the second half of summer. Combine the purple-veined 'Prince of Orange' with the scarlet 'Fire King', or contrast it with cooler colours such as those of bright blue, 'Blue Gem'. All make good cut flowers. Sow the seeds from early to late spring under glass, and grow in slightly acid, moist, free-draining soil.

OTHER VARIETIES Carnival Series (purple-veined, yellow, red, bronze-yellow, orange, pink or white flowers); 'Danish Flag' (red and white bicoloured flowers); 'National Ensign' (a bicoloured cultivar with deep pink-red and white flowers).

PLANT PROFILE

HEIGHT 20cm (8in)

SPREAD 15cm (6in)

SITE Full sun

SOIL Slightly acid, average, moist but free-draining

HARDINESS Half hardy

FLOWERING Mid- and late summer

N | *Nemophila maculata* Five-spot

THIS PLANT IS CALLED FIVE-SPOT because each white petal – of which there are five on each saucer-shaped flower – carries a distinctive violet-blue mark. The petals are also often faintly veined or tinted mauve. *N. maculata* is a diminutive plant with undeniable charms which is why it has become incredibly popular. It is often confused with baby blue-eyes (*N. menziesii*) which doesn't have the spots (see below). Both are well worth growing. Sow the seeds in spring where plants are to flower – once established they will self-seed. Grow in fertile, moist but free-draining soil.

OTHER VARIETY *N. menziesii* (bright blue flowers with dark blue markings and a pale centre).

PLANT PROFILE

HEIGHT 30cm (12in)

SPREAD 30cm (12in)

SITE Full sun or partial shade

SOIL Fertile, moist but free-draining

HARDINESS Half hardy

FLOWERING Summer

Nemophila menziesii 'Penny Black' Baby blue-eyes

N

WITH ITS SMALL, SKY-BLUE FLOWERS *N. menziesii* is a good choice for containers, rockeries and as an edging plant. But if you fancy something a bit more dramatic, grow 'Penny Black', with its white-edged, dark purple (almost black) flowers. Add pure white 'Snowstorm' for a striking display in a cottage-garden border. Sow the seeds in spring where plants are to flower, in fertile, moist but free-draining soil. Once established, plants self-seed freely.

OTHER VARIETIES *N. menziesii* subsp. *atromaria* (white flowers with black or dark purple spots); 'Oculata' (pale blue flowers with deep purple centres).

PLANT PROFILE
HEIGHT 20cm (8in)
SPREAD 30cm (12in)
SITE Full sun or partial shade
SOIL Fertile, moist but free-draining
HARDINESS Fully hardy
FLOWERING Summer

Nicandra physalodes Apple of Peru

ALSO KNOWN AS THE SHOO-FLY, the two common names of the multi-branching and fast-growing nicandra give three key pieces of information. First, it comes from South America; second, it has round green berries; and third, it is apparently a very effective fly repellent. What these common names do not reveal, however, is that its white-throated flowers don't last very long but replacements will keep being produced over a very long period from summer to the end of autumn. They are followed by berries enveloped in papery coats. Sow the seeds in spring under glass, and grow outside in fertile, moist but free-draining soil. Water well during dry spells.

OTHER VARIETY 'Violacea' (indigo-blue and white flowers).

PLANT PROFILE
HEIGHT 90cm (36in)
SPREAD 30cm (12in)
SITE Full sun
SOIL Fertile, moist but free-draining
HARDINESS Fully hardy
FLOWERING Summer to autumn

Nicotiana 'Havanna Apple Blossom' Tobacco plant

N

THE CHIEF VIRTUE of the Havanna Series is that the plants are compact – they are a great deal shorter than the 1.5m (5ft) spires of *N. sylvestris*. 'Havanna Apple Blossom' bears clusters of pink-tinged white flowers with a stronger pink on the underside of the petals. The plants are noted for their ability to withstand both hot and wet weather, and they perform reliably in the border and in containers. Sow the seeds from early to mid-spring under glass, and grow outside in fertile, moist but free-draining soil.

OTHER VARIETY Domino Series (flowers in red, white, crimson-pink, lime-green, pink with white eyes, purple, purple with white eyes, salmon-pink or white with rose-pink margins).

PLANT PROFILE
HEIGHT 35cm (14in)
SPREAD 40cm (16in)
SITE Full sun or partial shade
SOIL Fertile, moist but free-draining
HARDINESS Half hardy
FLOWERING Summer to autumn

N | *Nicotiana langsdorffii* Tobacco plant

IN SUMMER, THE APPLE-GREEN TUBULAR FLOWERS – up to 5cm (2in) long – of *N. langsdorffii* make a refreshing change from richer, more brightly coloured annuals. This is definitely not one of those bright and brash look-at-me-plants, yet its understated charms will certainly prove a real delight. The low-branching stems are sticky and hairy. Sow the seeds in mid-spring under glass, and grow outside in fertile, moist but free-draining soil.

OTHER VARIETY *N. alata* (tubular, greenish yellow flowers, with funnel-shaped mouths, which are white within).

PLANT PROFILE

HEIGHT 1.5m (5ft)

SPREAD 35cm (14in)

SITE Full sun or partial shade

SOIL Fertile, moist but free-draining

HARDINESS Half hardy

FLOWERING Summer to autumn

Nicotiana 'Lime Green' Tobacco plant

THE FRESH GREEN COLOURED FLOWERS of 'Lime Green' look striking in the summer border. Use them to break up leafy border areas of mid-green, or to provide a link into areas of stronger, richer colours. Bushy and multi-branching, this is a plant that looks best at the front of a border. It makes a nice change from the traditional, white-flowering *N. sylvestris* but its scent, which is released at night, is not as strong. Sow the seeds in mid-spring under glass, and grow outside in fertile, moist but free-draining soil.

OTHER VARIETY *N. sylvestris* (sweet-scented, long-tubed, trumpet-shaped white flowers).

PLANT PROFILE	
HEIGHT 60cm (24in)	
SPREAD 25cm (10in)	
SITE Full sun or partial shade	
SOIL Fertile, moist but free-draining	
HARDINESS Half hardy	
FLOWERING Midsummer to autumn	

N | *Nierembergia scoparia* 'Mont Blanc' Cup flower

GROWN AS AN ANNUAL in north-west Europe, this gem of a plant is actually a perennial from South America. The cup-shaped, lavender flowers, which have a distinctive yellow eye, look as though they are floating over the bright green, pointed foliage. Considering its beauty it gets surprisingly few mentions in gardening books. Place it at the front of the border or in a rock garden. Sow the seeds in spring under glass, and grow outside in moist but free-draining soil. To avoid sowing afresh each year, take stem-tip cuttings in summer and overwinter them in the conservatory or heated greenhouse.

OTHER VARIETY 'Purple Robe' (violet-blue flowers).

PLANT PROFILE

HEIGHT 20cm (8in)

SPREAD 20cm (8in)

SITE Full sun

SOIL Moist but free-draining

HARDINESS Half hardy

FLOWERING Summer

Nigella damascena 'Miss Jekyll' Love–in–a–mist

N

SKY-BLUE 'MISS JEKYLL' is still one of the best forms of love-in-a-mist. The plant has a frothy, cottage-garden feel about it with needle-thin leaves and double blooms that make long-lasting cut flowers. The seed pods may also be cut and dried. Incidentally, the common name is not a romantic poeticism but a graphic sexual euphemism for a woman's body. Sow the seeds in mid-spring or autumn where plants are to flower, in any free-draining soil. Once established it will readily self-seed.

OTHER VARIETIES 'Mulberry Rose' (rose-pink flowers); 'Oxford Blue' (large, double, dark blue flowers); 'Shorty Blue' (dark violet-blue flowers followed by decorative seed pods).

PLANT PROFILE

HEIGHT 45cm (18in)

SPREAD 23cm (9in)

SITE Full sun

SOIL Free-draining

HARDINESS Fully hardy

FLOWERING Late spring and early summer

SOOTHING SEEDS

The seeds of nigella are said to aid digestion and can be used in cooking. To extract them, just crush and sieve the contents of the ripe seedheads.

N *Nigella damascena* Persian Jewel Series Love-in-a-mist

NIGELLA GROWS IN ROCKY PLACES and fallow fields in Europe and North Africa, but it also looks fantastic in the cottage gardens of north-west Europe, where it is grown as a slender, stiffly upright, fast-growing annual. The solitary flowerheads of the Persian Jewel Series come in sky-blue, deep violet-blue, white, rose-pink or deep pink, each backed by a wispy, bright green 'ruff'. Its leaves, which are also bright green, are oval and finely cut. Sow the seeds in mid-spring where plants are to flower, in free-draining soil.

OTHER VARIETIES *N. damascena* (pale blue flowers, maturing to sky-blue); *N. hispanica* 'Curiosity' (scented, saucer-shaped, bright blue flowers); *N. orientalis* 'Transformer' (solitary, yellow flowers).

PLANT PROFILE	
HEIGHT 40cm (16in)	
SPREAD 23cm (9in)	
SITE Full sun	
SOIL Free-draining	
HARDINESS Fully hardy	
FLOWERING Late spring and early summer	

Nolana paradoxa 'Blue Bird'

N

THE TRUMPET-LIKE FLOWERS of 'Blue Bird' are sun worshippers and have a habit of closing up when the skies are grey. Mostly dark blue (although sometimes purple or purple-blue), they have a white throat which gradually turns yellow. For the best effect, grow them in blocks among plantings of impatiens (busy Lizzies), or other showy, summer annuals, or use them to form a circle of blue around a special feature, such as a statue or Ali Baba pot. Sow the seeds in early spring under glass, and grow outside in average soil.

OTHER VARIETY *N. humifusa* 'Little Bells' (lilac-blue flowers with broad white throats, streaked lilac-blue).

PLANT PROFILE	
HEIGHT 20cm (8in)	
SPREAD 60cm (24in)	
SITE Full sun	
SOIL Average	
HARDINESS Half hardy	
FLOWERING Summer	

MIXED HERBS

For maximum impact in the herb garden, plant rich purple 'Dark Opal' in geometric blocks or swirling patterns next to a bright green basil plant.

O

Ocimum basilicum var. *purpurascens* 'Dark Opal' Basil

SPECIALIST CATALOGUES NOW OFFER about 20 different kinds of basil. 'Dark Opal' is an especially attractive form with red–purple leaves – as well as being used in cooking, it makes a handsome foliage plant among mixed plantings of annuals. As soon as the soil has warmed up at the start of summer, sow the seeds of 'Dark Opal' where plants are to flower. The soil should be light, fertile and free draining. Cover seedlings with nets to stop pigeons eating the shoots. Remove flower buds as they appear to prevent leaves developing a bitter taste.

OTHER VARIETIES 'Genovese' (traditional Italian basil with large leaves); 'Green Ruffles' (large ruffled-edged leaves); 'Purple Ruffles' (fringed purple leaves).

PLANT PROFILE

HEIGHT 60cm (24in)

SPREAD 30cm (12in)

SITE Full sun

SOIL Light, fertile, free-draining

HARDINESS Half hardy

FLOWERING Late summer

Oenothera biennis Evening primrose

O

EVENING PRIMROSE IS A MUST in any garden, especially cottage and wildflower gardens. It makes a not-too-large, open-branched shape with bright yellow flowers that release the most wonderful fragrance in the evening. Sow the seeds in average soil in autumn, where plants are to flower, and keep it well watered in summer. Once established in the garden, plants will readily self-seed and new seedlings will pop up in the most surprising places.

OTHER VARIETIES *O. albicaulis* (spreading, bowl-shaped, scented flowers); *O. deltoides* (white, then pink flowers); *O. caespitosa* (smaller, scented); *O. fruticosa* (deep yellow flowers); *O. stricta* (smaller, scented).

PLANT PROFILE

HEIGHT 1.5m (5ft)	
SPREAD 60cm (24in)	
SITE Full sun	
SOIL Poor to moderately fertile, free-draining	
HARDINESS Fully hardy	
FLOWERING Summer to autumn	

O *Omphalodes linifolia* Venus's navelwort

IF YOU LOVE GYPSOPHILA, consider growing Venus's navelwort.
Like gypsophila it produces airy sprays of tiny white flowers in
the first half of summer, with the added bonus of a light fragrance.
Occasionally the blooms appear a very pale blue. The slender stems
and narrow, lance-shaped leaves are soft grey-green. You can
extend the flowering period by sowing two batches of seed: the
first in autumn to flower in spring, and the second in spring to
flower as the first batch is just finishing. Sow the seeds *in situ* in
average, free-draining soil. This plant will readily self-seed.

PLANT PROFILE

HEIGHT 40cm (16in)

SPREAD 15cm (6in)

SITE Full sun

SOIL Average, free-draining

HARDINESS Fully hardy

FLOWERING Spring to summer

Onopordum acanthium Cotton thistle

O

THE GIANT THISTLE ERUPTING out of the ground is one of the most impressive sights of the summer garden. It is an architectural plant on a grand scale with an erect central stem bearing wide branches of grey-green, spiny leaves up to 35cm (14in) long. Give it plenty of room both to grow and spread, and for you to stand back and admire it. Most people are so impressed by the foliage and stems that they don't seem to notice that its pale purple or white flowers aren't on the same scale. Sow the seeds in autumn or spring *in situ* in a wild garden or spare bed.

OTHER VARIETY *O. nervosum* (thistle-like, bright purple-red to purple-pink flowers).

PLANT PROFILE
HEIGHT 3m (10ft)
SPREAD 1m (3ft)
SITE Full sun
SOIL Neutral to slightly alkaline, fertile, free-draining
HARDINESS Fully hardy
FLOWERING Summer

O | *Orychophragmus violaceus*

A HARD-TO-FIND, RARELY GROWN ANNUAL, *O. violaceus* puts on a modest display of flowers which would suit the front of a cottage-garden border or an ornamental pot. The violet coloured blooms measure up to 2.5cm (1in) wide. At the base of the plant the leaves hug the ground, while higher up they clasp tightly to the stem. Sow the seeds *in situ* in spring or early summer in free-draining, fairly good soil in a sunny, sheltered position ready for flowering in early summer the following year. Alternatively, if you wish to grow it as a house or conservatory plant, sow the seeds in autumn under glass.

PLANT PROFILE

HEIGHT 60cm (24in)

SPREAD 30cm (12in)

SITE Sun

SOIL Fertile, free-draining

HARDINESS Half hardy

FLOWERING Late spring and early summer

Osteospermum 'Nairobi Purple'

THE OPEN, DAISY-LIKE FLOWERS of osteospermums appear over a long season – they are cheerful plants for the front of the border or edging a path. Many carry white flowers with a dark eye ('Silver Sparkler', for example) but 'Nairobi Purple' is in the pink-mauve-magenta range. It is among the more tender osteospermums and needs to be potted up in autumn and kept in a conservatory over winter as freezing temperatures or cold, wet soil will spell certain death. Sow the seeds in spring under glass, and grow outdoors in light, average, free-draining soil.

OTHER VARIETY 'Buttermilk' (primrose-yellow flowers).

PLANT PROFILE
HEIGHT To 45cm (18in)
SPREAD 90cm (36in)
SITE Full sun
SOIL Light, average, free-draining
HARDINESS Half hardy
FLOWERING Late spring to autumn

P | *Panicum capillare* Witch grass

NORTH AMERICAN WITCH GRASS is more modest than some of the blockbuster grasses, such as *Stipa gigantea* (golden oats) which grows up to 2.5m (8ft) high. With its lax, loosely tufted clumps of flat, lance-shaped, mid-green leaves, witch grass produces a hazy show of tiny spikelets on top of slender stems. It is a beautiful, gauzy plant for the front of a mixed border or in a mini meadow. Sow the seeds in spring on a warm windowsill or a greenhouse, and grow outdoors in average, free-draining soil.

PLANT PROFILE

HEIGHT 90cm (36in)

SPREAD 60cm (24in)

SITE Full sun

SOIL Average, free-draining

HARDINESS Half hardy

FLOWERING Late summer to autumn

Panicum miliaceum 'Violaceum' Millet

PROBABLY THE BEST FLOWERING ANNUAL GRASS, 'Violaceum' produces rigid heads of green flowers. These gradually droop under their own weight and turn purple-violet (the same colour as the leaves). For the biggest impact, grow it in small groups with other tall annual grasses. With its cob of edible yellow grain, the slender 2.4m (8ft) tall *Zea mays* (maize) would make an unusual backdrop to a border. Sow the seeds of 'Violaceum' in spring under glass, and grow outdoors in free-draining, average soil.

OTHER VARIETY *P. miliaceum* (slightly pendent, purple-tinged green flowers, borne in small spikelets).

PLANT PROFILE	
HEIGHT	90cm (36in)
SPREAD	23cm (9in)
SITE	Full sun
SOIL	Average, free-draining
HARDINESS	Fully hardy
FLOWERING	Late summer

P

Papaver commutatum 'Ladybird' Poppy

EASY-TO-GROW, 'LADYBIRD' puts on a bright show of bowl-shaped, crimson-red flowers with a bold black mark at the base of each petal. The 8cm (3in) wide blooms sit on top of long, thin stalks. It's always more of a pleasure than a nuisance when a plant as pretty as this self-seeds, guaranteeing a continued supply of flowers. Sow the seeds *in situ* in spring. In the wild, its parent plant, *P. commutatum*, grows in arid, rocky places and 'Ladybird' will grow likewise in any poor to moderately fertile soil so long as it is well drained.

OTHER VARIETY *P. commutatum* (solitary, bowl-shaped, brilliant red flowers).

PLANT PROFILE

HEIGHT 45cm (18in)

SPREAD 15cm (6in)

SITE Full sun

SOIL Poor to moderately fertile, free-draining

HARDINESS Fully hardy

FLOWERING Summer

Papaver nudicaule Arctic poppy

WITH THEIR SLENDER STEMS of paper thin, saucer-like flowers, these attractive annuals are most effective when grown in broad sweeps. The Arctic poppy (also known as the Icelandic poppy) is very different to the perennial *P. orientale* (Oriental poppy) which has a large clump of hairy leaves, and gigantic soup-bowl flowers. Arctic poppies are predominantly yellow or white but they can also be orange or pale red. They make a good, long-lasting cut flower. Sow the seeds in spring where plants are to flower, in poor to moderately fertile, free-draining soil.

OTHER VARIETY 'Summer Breeze' (orange, golden yellow, yellow, or white flowers over a very long period).

PLANT PROFILE
HEIGHT 30cm (12in)
SPREAD 15cm (6in)
SITE Full sun
SOIL Poor to moderately fertile, free-draining
HARDINESS Fully hardy
FLOWERING Summer

The dried seedheads of the Shirley Series can be sprayed or painted to add a contemporary, more vibrant look to dried-flower arrangements.

P

Papaver rhoeas Shirley Series **Field poppy**

THIS DELIGHTFUL TRIBE OF FLOWERS comes from one single wild flower which was originally spotted on waste ground in Surrey. Found by the Reverend W. Wilks in 1880, he went on to select, reselect and refine the colours until he created these double-flowered and single poppies (now available as semi-doubles and in other colours). What distinguishes them from other types is the lack of a black blotch at the base of the flower. The most popular colours have a petal fringe in a second shade. Sow the seeds in spring where plants are to flower, in poor to moderately fertile, free-draining soil.

OTHER VARIETY 'Mother of Pearl' (dove-grey, soft pink, or lilac-blue flowers with some paler zoning).

PLANT PROFILE

HEIGHT 60cm (24in)

SPREAD 30cm (12in)

SITE Full sun

SOIL Poor to moderately fertile, free-draining

HARDINESS Fully hardy

FLOWERING Summer

Papaver somniferum 'Paeony Flowered' Opium poppy

P

IGNORE THE NAME OPIUM because the narcotic, which is derived from the latex of the unripened seed capsules, is barely present in this garden variety. The seeds are perfectly safe and are wonderful sprinkled on bread before baking. It is also worth noting that the frilly flowers of 'Paeony Flowered' really do look like those of a peony. They are 10cm (4in) wide and sit on top of a long, straight stem of blue-green leaves. The large seed capsules are excellent in dried flower arrangements. Sow the seeds in spring where plants are to flower, in poor to moderately fertile, free-draining soil.

OTHER VARIETIES 'Hen and Chickens' (grown primarily for its ornamental seedheads); 'White Cloud' (double white flowers).

PLANT PROFILE
HEIGHT 1.2m (4ft)
SPREAD 30cm (12in)
SITE Full sun
SOIL Poor to moderately fertile, free-draining
HARDINESS Fully hardy
FLOWERING Summer

Pelargonium Horizon Series

PELARGONIUMS COME IN ALL SHAPES AND SIZES, from the 2m (6ft) tall, scented-leaved types to the multi-flowering, compact, bushy ones. The Horizon Series falls into the latter category, making the plants suitable for pots and the front of a border. They have a distinctive dark outer ring on their leaves and flowers that come in shades of pink, red ('Horizon Deep Scarlet' has the richest colour), and white. The plants will also hold up well during a wet summer. Sow the seeds in early spring under glass, and grow outdoors in fertile, free-draining soil. Bring under cover over winter.

OTHER VARIETIES Century Series (flowers in shades of red, pink, or white); Orbit Series (flowers in white or shades of pink, orange, or red).

PLANT PROFILE
HEIGHT 30cm (12in)
SPREAD 25cm (10in)
SITE Sun or partial shade
SOIL Neutral to alkaline, fertile, free-draining
HARDINESS Min 2°C (36°F)
FLOWERING Summer

Pelargonium 'Summer Showers'

P

THIS IVY-LEAVED, TRAILING PELARGONIUM is perfect for a hanging basket; but what goes down can, in this case, be trained to go up. In a large pot, plant four to six 'Summer Showers' around the base of a wigwam of canes and train the stems across and up, pinching out young shoots to encourage bushiness. By midsummer you will have a lovely display of flowers and evergreen leaves. Strong, dark colours, such as the purple-black 'Barbe Bleu', combine well with 'Summer Showers'. Sow the seeds in late winter or early spring under glass, and grow in fertile, free-draining soil. Bring under cover over winter.

OTHER VARIETIES 'Mme Crousse' (pale pink flowers borne in clusters); 'Rouletta' (bicoloured light crimson and white flowers).

PLANT PROFILE

HEIGHT 60cm (24in)

SPREAD 90cm (36in)

SITE Sun

SOIL Neutral to alkaline, fertile, free-draining

HARDINESS Min 2°C (36°F)

FLOWERING Summer

P

Pelargonium Tornado Series

IVY-LEAVED, EVERGREEN PELARGONIUMS are best grown in tall containers or hanging baskets so that their stems can trail over the sides. They also grow very well when supported with canes – this method is particularly good for displaying the striking flowers. The Tornado Series are particularly neat, compact plants with lilac and white flowers. They go well with purple-pink *P.* 'Leopard' and light purple *P.* 'Rhodamant'. Sow the seeds in late winter or early spring under glass, and plant outdoors in fertile, free-draining soil. Bring under cover in winter.

OTHER VARIETIES 'Amethyst' (purple and white flowers); 'Jackie' (pale lavender-pink flowers); 'Tavira' (light cerise-red flowers).

PLANT PROFILE

HEIGHT 25cm (10in)

SPREAD 20cm (8in)

SITE Sun

SOIL Neutral to alkaline, fertile, free-draining

HARDINESS Min 2°C (36°F)

FLOWERING Summer

Pericallis 'Brilliant' Florists' cineraria

THESE BRIGHT AND CHEERY Canary Island perennials form uniform cushions of long leaves with clusters of flowers held just above the foliage. Use them to fill gaps in the front of the border, or mix them with other annuals. Sow the seeds in late winter or early spring under glass, and grow outdoors in fertile, free-draining soil with some shade at midday. They also make wonderful pot-plant annuals for the house or conservatory, flowering from late winter to early spring – for this purpose, sow the seeds from spring to midsummer under glass and transfer the seedlings to larger pots.

OTHER VARIETY 'Chloe' (blue, carmine-red, pink and bicolour flowers).

PLANT PROFILE
HEIGHT 60cm (24in)
SPREAD 60cm (24in)
SITE Full sun with some midday shade
SOIL Fertile, free-draining
HARDINESS Min 7°C (45°C)
FLOWERING Summer

P | *Perilla frutescens* var. *crispa*

IT'S A RARE ANNUAL that can be used as a low hedge, and *P. frutescens* var. *crispa* quickly reaches a height of 60cm (24in) – usually it grows taller. It is a sumptuous foliage plant with 12cm (5in) long, frilly-edged, dark purple leaves, similar to those of a large basil plant. They make the perfect backdrop for anything white, yellow or orange. The whorled spikes of tiny white flowers are not in the same league, however, and are best snipped off so that they don't distract from the main event. Sow the seeds in spring under glass, and grow outdoors in fertile, moist but free-draining soil.

OTHER VARIETY *P. frutescens* (green, sometimes purple flecked leaves and whorls of tiny white flowers borne in spikes).

PLANT PROFILE

HEIGHT 1m (3ft)

SPREAD 30cm (12in)

SITE Full sun or partial shade

SOIL Fertile, moist but free-draining

HARDINESS Frost hardy

FLOWERING Summer

Petroselinum crispum 'Afro' Parsley

P

THERE ARE TWO KINDS OF PARSLEY: flat, plain leaved (the Italian form has a stronger taste than the French) and the tightly bunched. The latter, into which category *P. crispum* 'Afro' falls, is by far the most attractive on the plate and in the garden. Rather than being confined to the kitchen garden, it deserves its place as a decorative plant for the front of a mixed border. Remove the flower stems as soon as they appear or the supply of leaves will falter. Sow the seeds (which are slow to germinate) in spring where plants are to grow, in fertile, moist but free-draining soil with some shade.

OTHER VARIETY 'Clivi' (compact, with dark green leaves).

PLANT PROFILE
HEIGHT 80cm (32in)
SPREAD 60cm (24in)
SITE Sun with some shade
SOIL Fertile, moist but free-draining
HARDINESS Fully hardy
FLOWERING Summer of second year

P

Petunia 'Lavender Storm'

THE PETUNIAS IN THE GRANDIFLORA GROUP to which 'Lavender Storm' belongs, generally have fewer flowers than some other petunias but the large size of the blooms more than makes up for this shortfall. The only problem is that they can take quite a beating in heavy rain, although this particular variety survives better than most in the group. Sow the seeds in mid-spring or autumn under glass, and grow outdoors in light, free-draining soil with shelter from strong winds.

OTHER VARIETY Dream Series (white, pink, salmon-pink, magenta, or red flowers).

PLANT PROFILE	
HEIGHT	30cm (12in)
SPREAD	30cm (12in)
SITE	Full sun
SOIL	Light, free-draining
HARDINESS	Half hardy
FLOWERING	Summer

Petunia 'Purple Wave'

'PURPLE WAVE' BELONGS TO THE MULTIFLORA GROUP which means that it produces prodigious numbers of flowers up to 5cm (2in) wide on a bushy plant. It has brilliant magenta trumpets with a dark centre and is different from most petunias in the group because it is a vigorous spreader with a trailing habit. Sow the seeds in mid-spring or autumn under glass, and grow outdoors in light, free-draining soil with shelter from wind.

OTHER VARIETIES Mirage Series (large flowers in white, or shades of blue, pink, red or purple, some with darker veining or central stars); Primetime Series (compact, flowers stand up well in heavy rain).

PLANT PROFILE
HEIGHT 45cm (18in)
SPREAD 90cm (36in)
SITE Full sun
SOIL Light, free-draining
HARDINESS Half hardy
FLOWERING Summer

P | *Phacelia campanularia* Californian bluebell

THE DARK BLUE COLOUR of the flowers of *P. campanularia* is rarely found in annuals (they also come in white), and the upward-pointing bell shape is also quite distinct. These two unusual features make it an eye-catching plant for the front of a border or rockery. Californian bluebells are satisfyingly fast to germinate and will be ready to flower just eight weeks after sowing. It is important to sow the seeds in spring or early autumn where they are to flower because the plants hate being moved. They prefer fertile, free-draining soil.

OTHER VARIETY *P. tanacetifolia* (bell-shaped, lavender-blue or blue flowers).

PLANT PROFILE

HEIGHT 30cm (12in)

SPREAD 15cm (6in)

SITE Full sun

SOIL Fertile, free-draining

HARDINESS Fully hardy

FLOWERING Late spring and summer

Phlox drummondii Annual phlox

P

THE FLOWERS OF ANNUAL PHLOX may be small at just 2.5cm (1in) across, but they appear in decent-sized clusters that last a week, with plenty of replacements waiting in the wings. This steady stream of flowers goes on right through summer. Improve bushiness and flower production by nipping off the growing tips. *P. drummondii* has many first-rate cultivars (see below). Sow the seeds in early spring under glass, and grow outdoors in fertile, free-draining soil.

OTHER VARIETIES 'African Sunset' (intense red flowers with a white eye); 'Brilliant' (pink flowers); 'Chanal' (almost rose-like, pink flowers); Ethnie Pastel Shades Series (very short); 'Sternenzauber' (small, star-like flowers in various shades, mainly pink).

PLANT PROFILE

HEIGHT 45cm (18in)

SPREAD 25cm (10in)

SITE Full sun

SOIL Fertile, free-draining

HARDINESS Frost hardy

FLOWERING Summer

P

Platystemon californicus Californian poppy

ALSO KNOWN AS CREAMCUPS, the Californian poppy comes from the hot, dry, desert margins of western North America where it enjoys light, free-draining soil and plenty of sun. A gravel or rock garden, or a Mediterranean-style garden would be the perfect home for it. It is a multi-branching plant with 8cm (3in) long, grey-tinged green leaves and, in late spring, charming six-petalled flowers on the pale, creamy side of yellow. Sow the seeds in early spring where the plants are to flower, avoiding rich soil at all costs.

PLANT PROFILE	
HEIGHT 30cm (12in)	
SPREAD 23cm (9in)	
SITE Full sun	
SOIL Light, free-draining	
HARDINESS Fully hardy	
FLOWERING Late spring	

Plectranthus thyrsoideus

P

IN ITS NATIVE AFRICA *P. thyrsoideus* makes a branching, shrubby plant, but in north-west Europe, where it is grown as an annual, the growing season isn't long enough for it to reach anywhere near that size. With its bright blue flowers, upright growth and attractive, heart-shaped, hairy green leaves it makes a wonderful summer bedder and container plant; it will also grow happily as a house or conservatory. Sow the seeds in spring under glass, and grow outdoors in average, free-draining soil.

OTHER VARIETIES *P. amboinicus* (whorled, tubular, two-lipped, lilac-pink, mauve or white flowers); *P. argentatus* (whorled, tubular, pale blue-white flowers); *P. forsteri* (whorled, tubular, pale mauve or white flowers).

PLANT PROFILE
HEIGHT 90cm (36in)
SPREAD 60cm (24in)
SITE Dappled shade
SOIL Average, free-draining
HARDINESS Min 4°C (39°F)
FLOWERING Summer

P *Polypogon monspeliensis* Beard grass

ALSO KNOWN AS RABBIT'S FOOT GRASS, the silky, bristly spikelets of this clump-forming annual look good at the front of borders or in wildflower gardens. The narrow seedheads appear during summer and autumn and age from green to soft beige-brown. When cut and dried they look wonderful in flower arrangements. The mid-green leaves are flat, narrow and rough. Sow the seeds *in situ* in spring or autumn. Beard grass is a native of European grasslands and should, therefore, be grown in light, free-draining, average soil.

PLANT PROFILE

HEIGHT 60cm (24in)

SPREAD 20cm (8in)

SITE Sun

SOIL Average, free-draining

HARDINESS Fully hardy

FLOWERING Summer to autumn

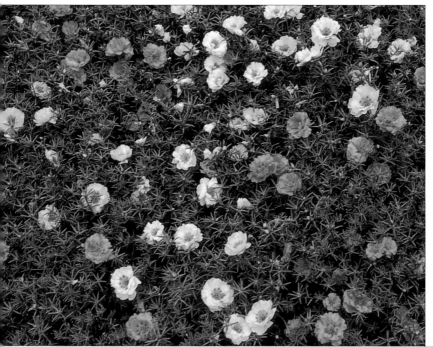

Portulaca grandiflora Sundial Series **Purslane**

P

IN THE PAST, this fleshy-leaved, prostrate plant with its satiny flowers and red stems has attracted many admirers, but because it needed long, hot summers to perform well few people tried growing it. The new Sundial Series, however, has been bred to grow in cooler conditions. The plants bear double flowers in a wide colour range, and some are striped and flecked with lavender-blue – the shape of the blooms explains its other common name of rose moss. Sow the seeds under glass in spring, and grow outdoors in poor, sandy, free-draining soil – the front of a raised bed or in pots is ideal.

OTHER VARIETY Sundance Hybrids (semi-trailing, with large, semi-double or double flowers).

PLANT PROFILE
HEIGHT 25cm (10in)
SPREAD 15cm (6in)
SITE Full sun
SOIL Poor, sandy, free-draining
HARDINESS Half hardy
FLOWERING Summer

P | *Primula* Cowichan Series **Primrose**

ALWAYS GIVING A STRONG SHOW – although the weather can be at its worst during the run-up to spring – the Cowichan Series produces velvety flowers in a range of rich reds, purples, maroons, blues, or yellows. The plants also make sturdy rosettes of heavily veined, oval-shaped, dark green leaves. Sow the seeds in spring in a cold frame, and plant outdoors in reliably moist but free-draining, average to fertile soil to flower the following winter.

OTHER VARIETIES Crescendo Series (large, yellow-centred flowers); Rainbow Series (yellow-centred flowers in blue, creamy-yellow, pink, carmine-red, scarlet-red, white or yellow, plus unusual rusty orange).

PLANT PROFILE

HEIGHT 30cm (12in)

SPREAD 30cm (12in)

SITE Partial shade

SOIL Average, moist but free-draining

HARDINESS Fully hardy

FLOWERING Winter to spring

Primula 'Wanda' Primrose

P

ONE OF THE BEST and most easily grown primroses, the evergreen or semi-evergreen 'Wanda' will keep flowering from late winter until the end of spring. For the best effect, grow plants in big blocks to produce a strong swathe of colour. Although it grows perfectly well in light shade, it flowers longer and more abundantly in full sun; too much shade will give more leaves than flowers. Sow the seeds in late winter or early spring in a cold frame, and plant outdoors in average to fertile, moist but free-draining soil to flower the following winter.

OTHER VARIETY Wanda Supreme Series (flowers in shades of blue, yellow, purple, burgundy, red, rose, and pink bicolours).

PLANT PROFILE
HEIGHT 15cm (6in)
SPREAD 40cm (16in)
SITE Sun or partial shade
SOIL Average, moist but free-draining
HARDINESS Fully hardy
FLOWERING Late winter to late spring

P *Proboscidea louisianica* Ram's horn

WHITE, FOXGLOVE-LIKE FLOWERS and diamond-shaped mid-green leaves make *P. louisianica* a rather attractive plant. But two things make it an exceptional one: first, the distinctive maroon markings on the funnel-shaped blooms; and second, the curious boat-shaped fruit that follow. These are about 15cm (6in) in length with long horn-like growths – hence the descriptive common name of ram's horn. Sow the seeds in spring under glass, and plant out in fertile, moist but well-drained soil.

OTHER VARIETY *P. fragrans* (funnel-shaped, fragrant, red-purple to purple flowers).

PLANT PROFILE

HEIGHT 60cm (24in)

SPREAD 30cm (12in)

SITE Full sun

SOIL Fertile, moist but free-draining

HARDINESS Half hardy

FLOWERING Summer

Psylliostachys suworowii Statice

STATICE IS A GOOD CHOICE FOR SEASIDE GARDENS. From a ground-hugging rosette of long, wavy-margined leaves, it sends up 20cm (8in) long, branching flower spikes that are covered with tiny pink blooms and look like sugar-coated wands. The flower spikes are excellent for cutting and can be used in fresh or dried flower arrangements. Sow the seeds in spring under glass, or late spring *in situ*, and grow outdoors in fertile, moist but well-drained soil. Perfect settings include a sunny, sheltered gravel garden or raised bed.

OTHER VARIETY *P. spicata* (rose-pink flowers).

PLANT PROFILE
HEIGHT 45cm (18in)
SPREAD 30cm (12in)
SITE Full sun
SOIL Fertile, moist but free-draining
HARDINESS Half hardy
FLOWERING Summer to early autumn

R | *Ratibida pinnata* Drooping coneflower

STRONG, ERECT AND MULTI-BRANCHING, this perennial is also often grown as an annual or biennial. At the end of summer, when the rest of the garden is beginning to slow down, the drooping coneflower will still provide a shot of colour. The daisy-like flowers are 12cm (5in) across, with a prominent red-brown, cone-shaped eye. If you pinch a flower at the base of its petals it will release a strong scent of aniseed. The leaves are an attractive bluish-green. Sow the seeds at the start of spring in pots in a cold frame; because it is drought-resistant and likes average, free-draining soil, plant it outdoors in a gravel garden or dry border.

OTHER VARIETY *R. columnifera* (yellow, brown and green flowers).

PLANT PROFILE

HEIGHT 1.2m (4ft)

SPREAD 45cm (18in)

SITE Full sun

SOIL Neutral to slightly alkaline, average, free-draining

HARDINESS Fully hardy

FLOWERING Summer to autumn

Rehmannia elata Chinese foxglove

R

WITH FLOWERS EASILY MISTAKEN FOR A FOXGLOVE, *R. elata* is a bushy plant with branching stems that produces pink-purple tubular flowers with red-freckled throats. Unless you can give it a sunny, sheltered, frost-free spot in fertile but free-draining soil it won't be reliably hardy, and is best dug up in autumn, cut back and potted up for overwintering in a cool greenhouse. Water sparingly. Plant out again the following spring after the last frost. Sow the seeds in late winter under glass – seedlings take 12–14 months to flower.

OTHER VARIETY *R. glutinosa* (flowers have red-brown tubes, marked with darker red-purple veins, and pale yellow-brown lips).

PLANT PROFILE

HEIGHT 1.5m (5ft)

SPREAD 50cm (20in)

SITE Full sun

SOIL Fertile, free-draining

HARDINESS Borderline hardy

FLOWERING Late spring to midsummer

R | *Reseda odorata* Common mignonette

FOUND GROWING AS A WEED IN EGYPT, the common mignonette became a European cottage-garden favourite due to its sweet raspberry fragrance. A magnet for bees, the scent lingers even when the flowers are cut and dried. While it may be a veritable perfume factory, it isn't the prettiest of plants, so tuck it away in the border surrounded by attractive, possibly scentless, neighbours. Modern cultivars have been developed with more eye-catching blooms but annoyingly, the strength of the fragrance has been lost. Sow the seeds in late winter under glass, or *in situ* in early spring and autumn in preferably alkaline, free-draining soil.

OTHER VARIETY 'True Machet' (red-tinged, highly fragrant flowers).

PLANT PROFILE

HEIGHT 60cm (24in)

SPREAD 23cm (9in)

SITE Full sun or light shade

SOIL Preferably alkaline, free-draining

HARDINESS Fully hardy

FLOWERING Summer to early autumn

Rhodanthe chlorocephala subsp. *rosea* Strawflower

R

IN ITS NATIVE AUSTRALIA this plant is called the everlasting flower because its striking, daisy-like blooms last for ages on the plant. They have a papery texture that makes them perfect for dried flower arrangements: pick them just before they have fully opened and hang them upside down to dry in a cool, shady, airy place. The colours should last for at least nine months. The flowers also display an unusual habit of closing up tightly when the sky is overcast. Sow the seeds in early spring under glass, or in mid-spring where plants are to flower in poor, light, free-draining soil.

OTHER VARIETY *R. manglesii* (daisy-like flowers with red, pink or white bracts).

PLANT PROFILE	
HEIGHT 60cm (24in)	
SPREAD 15cm (6in)	
SITE Full sun	
SOIL Light, free-draining	
HARDINESS Half hardy	
FLOWERING Summer	

R

Rhodochiton atrosanguineus

AN EXOTIC CLIMBER FROM MEXICO, *R. atrosanguineus* has almost black, bell-shaped flowers with a protruding maroon tube. When trained up pergolas, trellis or over adjoining shrubs in a cool, sunny (with some shade from the midday sun) and sheltered position, it should keep on producing flowers until halted by the first frost. Sow the seeds in spring on a windowsill or in a greenhouse, and grow outdoors in moist but free-draining, fertile soil. Pot-grown plants are best brought into a cool greenhouse or conservatory for the winter.

PLANT PROFILE

HEIGHT 3m (10ft)

SITE Full sun with shade from midday sun

SOIL Average, moist but free-draining

HARDINESS Min 3–5°C (37–41°F)

FLOWERING Summer to autumn

All parts of this plant are highly toxic if ingested, so it's best to avoid it in gardens where children play. Its foliage can cause skin allergies.

Ricinus communis 'Carmencita' Castor oil plant

R

MAKE 'CARMENCITA' THE KEY FEATURE in a display of architectural plants, where its spikes of red female flowers and handsome dark bronze-red, hand-like leaves – up to 30cm (12in) long – will inject a tropical lushness. It goes particularly well with palms, banana trees and cannas. In late spring, sow the seeds (pre-soaked for 24 hours) at a temperature of 21°C (71°F); pot on seedlings and grow at 13°C (55°F). Keep potting on until plants are almost bursting out of 20cm (8in) pots; then, after the last frost, plant them out in fertile, free-draining soil. Shelter is vital to avoid wind damage to the leaves.

OTHER VARIETIES 'Red Spire' (taller growing, red stems and bronze-flushed leaves); 'Zanzibarensis' (taller, white-veined, mid-green leaves).

PLANT PROFILE

HEIGHT	2m (6ft)
SPREAD	1m (3ft)
SITE	Full sun
SOIL	Fertile, free-draining
HARDINESS	Half hardy
FLOWERING	Summer

Rudbeckia hirta 'Rustic Dwarfs' Black-eyed Susan

THESE SHORT-LIVED PERENNIALS are best grown as late-flowering annuals. Their strong marmalade colours will boost a flagging garden when so many other plants have finished flowering. 'Rustic Dwarfs' are particularly colourful, with a brown-purple centre and golden yellow, brown-red or bronze-orange petals, some of which are bicoloured. Sow the seeds in spring under glass, and grow outdoors in a warm, sheltered spot in slightly heavy, moist soil – the stems will quickly collapse if the soil is allowed to bake dry.

OTHER VARIETIES 'Bambi' (bronze-brown, chestnut-brown, and golden yellow flowers); 'Marmalade' (bushy and compact with large, deep golden-orange flowers).

PLANT PROFILE

HEIGHT 60cm (24in)

SPREAD 35cm (14in)

SITE Full sun or partial shade

SOIL Slightly heavy, free-draining, should not dry out

HARDINESS Fully hardy

FLOWERING Summer to early autumn

Salpiglossis sinuata Bolero Hybrids

S

DURING A LONG, HOT SUMMER this is one of the best-performing annuals with exotic, heavily veined flowers in a range of bright, striking colours. If the summer is cold and wet, however, it not only looks dreadful, but also gives off a rather unpleasant, rotting smell. The answer is to grow Bolero Hybrids in containers in the conservatory or on a sunny porch. Don't crowd the pots together or the plants will become straggly. If you want a border plant, then you will be better off choosing a more weather-resistant strain, such as the compact Casino Series. Sow the seeds in mid-spring under glass, and in moist but free-draining soil or compost.

OTHER VARIETY 'Kew Blue' (purple-blue, heavily veined flowers).

PLANT PROFILE
HEIGHT 60cm (24in)
SPREAD 30cm (12in)
SITE Full sun
SOIL Moist but free-draining
HARDINESS Half hardy
FLOWERING Summer to autumn

S

Salvia argentea Sage

THIS SHORT-LIVED SALVIA is grown more for its silvery-grey foliage than its pinkish-white flowers which are rather insignificant. The leaves are 20cm (8in) long with a covering of silky hairs which makes them delightfully woolly – slugs, unfortunately, adore them. Many gardeners prefer to remove the flowers because, if allowed to develop, they cause the leaves to turn grey-green, but it won't hurt to leave one or two flowers to self-seed and so ensure next year's display. Alternatively, sow the seeds in a cold frame in summer for flowering the following year, and grow outdoors in fertile soil that is moist but well-drained.

OTHER VARIETY *S. aethiopis* (white or yellow-lipped flowers).

PLANT PROFILE

HEIGHT 90cm (36in)

SPREAD 60cm (24in)

SITE Full sun or light shade

SOIL Fertile, moist but free-draining

HARDINESS Fully hardy

FLOWERING Mid- and late summer

Salvia coccinea 'Lady in Red' Sage

S

ERECT AND BUSHY, 'Lady in Red' has characteristic two-lipped salvia flowers ranged in tiers up the slender flower stem. It is a good choice if you want a self-seeding red which is not as strident as some salvias. Grow it in formal schemes with blocks or strands of intermingling colour, or use it to cover the low bare stems of climbing roses. It mixes particularly well with two other cultivars: the white 'Snow Nymph' and the coral-pink 'Coral Nymph'. Sow the seeds in mid-spring under glass, and grow outdoors in fertile, moist but free-draining soil.

OTHER VARIETY 'Starry Eyed' (white, red or coral-pink flowers).

PLANT PROFILE

HEIGHT 40cm (16in)

SPREAD 23cm (9in)

SITE Full sun or partial shade

SOIL Fertile, moist but free-draining

HARDINESS Half hardy

FLOWERING Summer to autumn

Salvia farinacea 'Victoria' Mealy sage

WITHIN JUST FOUR MONTHS of sowing you will get the deep blue flower spikes and narrow glossy, green leaves of 'Victoria' and the plant continues to bush out as summer progresses. Mealy sage gets its name from the curious white covering on its stems – *farinacea* is Latin for flour. The flowers are particularly good for cutting and they also dry well for use in winter arrangements. Sow the seeds in mid-spring under glass, and grow outdoors in fertile, moist but free-draining soil.

OTHER VARIETIES *S. farinacea* (deep lavender-blue flowers); 'Rhea' (compact, early dark blue flowers); 'Strata' (blue and white flowers); 'White Porcelain' (white flowers).

PLANT PROFILE

HEIGHT 60cm (24in)

SPREAD 30cm (12in)

SITE Full sun or partial shade

SOIL Fertile, moist but free-draining

HARDINESS Half hardy

FLOWERING Summer to autumn

Salvia officinalis 'Tricolor' Common sage

AN ESSENTIAL PLANT FOR A SUNNY GARDEN, sage has powerfully aromatic leaves (rub them and sniff). It makes a lovely bushy plant. With its pink, cream, and purple marked leaves, 'Tricolor' is much more colourful than its plain green parent, *S. officinalis*. Young plants will need protection in their first few winters: either grow them in a sunny sheltered site, or keep them in pots to make it easier to move them under cover over winter. Sow the seeds in mid-spring under glass, and grow outdoors in fertile, moist but free-draining soil – leaving plants in cold, saturated soil over winter is the quickest way to kill them.

OTHER VARIETY 'Purpurascens' (red-purple young leaves).

PLANT PROFILE
HEIGHT 80cm (32in)
SPREAD 1m (3ft)
SITE Full sun or partial shade
SOIL Fertile, moist but free-draining
HARDINESS Fully hardy
FLOWERING Early and midsummer

S

S | *Salvia splendens* Cleopatra Series Scarlet sage

A PARTICULARLY LIVELY SCARLET SAGE, the flowers of the Cleopatra Series are not only red, they also come in salmon-pink, purple or white. As with all cultivars of its parent plant, *S. splendens*, the Cleopatra Series produces erect, bushy perennials, more usually grown as annuals. The leaves are oval, toothed and slightly hairy. In mid-spring, sow the seeds (encourage germination by pre-soaking them) in pots on a windowsill or in a greenhouse, and grow outdoors in fertile, moist but free-draining soil.

OTHER VARIETY 'Red Arrow' (very dark green leaves, scarlet flowers).

PLANT PROFILE

HEIGHT 40cm (16in)

SPREAD 25cm (10in)

SITE Full sun or light shade

SOIL Fertile, moist but free-draining

HARDINESS Half hardy

FLOWERING Summer to autumn

Salvia splendens 'Scarlet King' Scarlet sage

S

A BRASH, BRIGHT FIRECRACKER of a plant, 'Scarlet King' is just what you need for a hot coloured border. It can be used with other upbeat plants in a massed display or in small groups for shock value. Either way, the colour can't be rivalled. By nipping off the growing tips you can encourage the plant to bush out and produce extra flower stems. In mid-spring, sow the seeds (pre-soaking will aid germination) under glass, and grow outdoors in fertile, moist but free-draining soil.

OTHER VARIETY Sizzler Series (early flowers in bright shades of cerise-red, lavender-blue, salmon-pink, purple, scarlet or white).

PLANT PROFILE
HEIGHT 25cm (10in)
SPREAD 20cm (8in)
SITE Full sun or partial shade
SOIL Fertile, moist but free-draining
HARDINESS Half hardy
FLOWERING Summer to autumn

S *Salvia viridis* **Annual clary**

IT COMES AS A REAL SURPRISE TO LEARN that what look like the pinkish-purple, papery flowers of *S. viridis* are not flowers at all but long growths; the true flowers are the tiny two-lipped clusters of cream and purple-tipped petals hidden away beneath them. Annual clary is an upright, bushy plant that's ideal for informal, cottage gardens. It also makes a good cut flower that dries well for winter displays. Sow the seeds in mid-spring under glass, and grow outdoors in fertile, moist but free-draining soil.

OTHER VARIETIES 'Oxford Blue' (violet blue); 'Pink Sundae' (rosy-red cottage-garden favourite); 'White Swan' (white bracts with green veins).

PLANT PROFILE
HEIGHT 50cm (20in)
SPREAD 23cm (9in)
SITE Full sun or partial shade
SOIL Fertile, moist but free-draining
HARDINESS Fully hardy
FLOWERING Summer

Sanvitalia procumbens Creeping zinnia

S

RELIABLE AND ATTRACTIVE but still not as popular as it should be, creeping zinnia can be used in all kinds of ways – as ground cover, edging (for paths and patios), in troughs and hanging baskets, as well as at the front of a border. It is a low-growing, mat-forming plant that creeps across the ground producing miniature sunflower-like blooms (bright yellow petals surrounding a black centre). Sow the seeds in autumn or spring where plants are to flower, in fertile, free-draining soil.

OTHER VARIETIES 'Gold Braid' (shorter-growing, golden-yellow flowers); 'Golden Carpet' (dwarf, lemon-yellow flowers); 'Mandarin Orange' (semi-double, orange flowers).

PLANT PROFILE
HEIGHT 20cm (8in)
SPREAD 45cm (18in)
SITE Full sun
SOIL Fertile, free-draining
HARDINESS Fully hardy
FLOWERING Early summer to early autumn

S | *Satureja hortensis* Summer savory

A PRETTY HERB WITH A PUNGENT FLAVOUR, summer savory goes well with meat dishes and stuffings but is best used sparingly. It is also traditionally used with beans because it is said to counter flatulence. The bushy plants are liberally covered with lance-shaped, fresh green leaves and small pink or white flowers that are attractive to bees. Not the most dazzling subject for a flower border, it is a must for the herb garden. Sow the seeds in late winter or early spring in pots on the windowsill or in a greenhouse, and grow outdoors in neutral to slightly alkaline, well-drained soil.

OTHER VARIETY *S. montana* (winter savory has an even stronger flavour and pink-purple flowers).

PLANT PROFILE
HEIGHT 25cm (10in)
SPREAD 30cm (12in)
SITE Full sun
SOIL Neutral to slightly alkaline, free-draining
HARDINESS Frost hardy
FLOWERING Summer

Scabiosa atropurpurea Pincushion flower

S

THE BEE- AND BUTTERFLY-ATTRACTING FLOWERS of this plant really do look like small pincushions perched on top of thin, wiry stems. They are highly valued by flower arrangers because they last nearly two weeks in water – it is worth growing a few extra plants specifically for cutting. The Cockade Series comes in shades of red, purple, pink or blue. Sow the seeds in early spring under glass, or in mid-spring where plants are to flower. For best results grow in neutral to slightly alkaline, free-draining soil. Deadheading will prolong flowering.

OTHER VARIETIES 'Blue Cockade' (lavender-blue to purple-blue flowers); 'Dwarf Double' (double flowers in white, purple, blue or pink).

PLANT PROFILE
HEIGHT 90cm (36in)
SPREAD 23cm (9in)
SITE Full sun
SOIL Neutral to slightly alkaline, free-draining
HARDINESS Fully hardy
FLOWERING Summer

S *Scabiosa stellata* 'Paper Moon' Pincushion flower

THE FLOWERS OF 'PAPER MOON' are typically scabious-like with clusters of tiny petals on top of wiry, branching stems. Pleasant enough… but it's the seed heads that make this such an extraordinary plant. These round, parchment-brown pompons with their interesting cup-shaped hollow bracts are sculptural delights and excellent for drying. Sow the seeds in early spring under glass, or in mid-spring where plants are to flower, in neutral to slightly alkaline, average, free-draining soil.

OTHER VARIETIES 'Drum Stick' (shorter growing, light blue flowers, turning bronze); 'Ping Pong' (bears small white seed heads).

PLANT PROFILE

HEIGHT 45cm (18in)

SPREAD 23cm (9in)

SITE Full sun

SOIL Neutral to slightly alkaline, average, free-draining

HARDINESS Fully hardy

FLOWERING Summer

Scaevola aemula Fairy fan-flower

S

A TENDER, EVERGREEN PERENNIAL, *S. aemula* is often treated as an annual. It is has spoon-shaped leaves and tiny summer flowers with five petals that spread out to form a semi-circular fan. A trailing habit makes it suitable for hanging baskets or containers. Try a mixed planting with the white 'Alba'. Sow the seeds in spring under glass, but wait until all risk of frost has passed before planting out in fertile, moist but free-draining soil. Plants grown in the border should be dug up and placed in pots to overwinter in a cool greenhouse or conservatory.

OTHER VARIETIES 'Blue Fan' (blue flowers with a white eye); 'Blue Wonder' (lilac-blue flowers, shorter but more spreading, free flowering).

PLANT PROFILE

HEIGHT 50cm (20in)

SPREAD 50cm (20in)

SITE Full sun or light dappled shade

SOIL Fertile, moist but free-draining

HARDINESS Min 5°C (41°F)

FLOWERING Summer

S

Schizanthus pinnatus 'Hit Parade' Poor man's orchid

THIS ORCHID LOOKALIKE is actually a relative of the tomato plant. From South America, *S. pinnatus* is an upright, bushy plant (even bushier if you nip off the growing tips on young plants) with finely divided, fern-like leaves. The distinctive flowers of 'Hit Parade', which are popular with flower arrangers, come in yellow, pink, white, red or purple, often with a contrasting yellow throat speckled with violet. Sow the seeds in mid-spring under glass, and grow outdoors in fertile, very free-draining soil in a warm, sheltered spot.

OTHER VARIETIES Giant Hybrids (taller at 1.2m, 4ft); *S. pinnatus* (white, yellow, pink, purple or red flowers, often with yellow throats and violet markings).

PLANT PROFILE
HEIGHT 50cm (20in)
SPREAD 30cm (12in)
SITE Full sun
SOIL Fertile, very free-draining
HARDINESS Min 5°C (41°F)
FLOWERING Spring to autumn

Schizanthus pinnatus 'Star Parade' Poor man's orchid

S

A COMPACT AND PRETTY ANNUAL, 'Star Parade' has a distinctive pyramidal habit. Its flowers emerge from spring to autumn and are backed by fern-like, light green leaves that are about 12cm (5in) long. Sow the seeds in mid-spring on a windowsill or in a greenhouse. Originally from the dry, rocky slopes of Chile, *S. pinnatus* and its cultivars, including 'Star Parade', should be grown in fertile, very free-draining soil. A wonderful house and conservatory plant, it also grows well outside in a warm, sheltered site. The flowers are excellent for cutting.

OTHER VARIETY *S. x wisetonensis* (taller growing, white, pale blue, pink or red-brown flowers).

PLANT PROFILE
HEIGHT 25cm (10in)
SPREAD 30cm (12in)
SITE Full sun
SOIL Fertile, very free-draining
HARDINESS Min 5°C (41°F)
FLOWERING Spring to autumn

S | *Sedum caeruleum* Stonecrop

IN ITS NATIVE HABITAT, the creeping, mat-forming stonecrop can be found growing in hot, dry, sunny places on rocky ground. To do well in colder climates it must be planted in full sun in poor, light, free-draining soil. Its diminutive size calls for a place on the top of a dry-stone wall or in gaps in patio paving – in these situations not only will the plant be seen clearly, it will have the perfect growing conditions. The tiny, star-shaped flowers are the palest blue and appear on the tips of the fleshy pale green leaves (these redden with age). Sow the seeds in early spring in pots on a windowsill or in a greenhouse, or in late spring where plants are to flower.

OTHER VARIETY *S. pilosum* (rose-red, bell-shaped flowers).

PLANT PROFILE
HEIGHT 15cm (6in)
SPREAD 15cm (6in)
SITE Full sun
SOIL Poor, light, free-draining
HARDINESS Fully hardy
FLOWERING Summer

Sedum sempervivoides Stonecrop

S

A ROCKERY OR TOP OF A DRY STONE WALL are ideal situations for this mat-forming plant because it is so small it would be lost anywhere else, except in containers. It also demands excellent drainage. The neatly whorled rosettes of leaves are a soft blue-green with a red tinge at the base – slugs and snails adore them, so keep a look out for these pests. In summer it bears small clusters of red star-shaped flowers. Sow the seeds in pots on a windowsill or in a greenhouse in early spring to flower the following year, or sow them in mid-spring where plants are to flower in average soil.

PLANT PROFILE

HEIGHT 10cm (4in)

SPREAD 15cm (6in)

SITE Full sun

SOIL Average, very free-draining

HARDINESS Frost hardy

FLOWERING Summer

SUGARY MIX

The dramatic foliage of 'Silver Dust' takes on a more delicate quality when it's planted in pots with soft, sugary pinks and raspberry shades.

S

Senecio cineraria 'Silver Dust'

AN ESSENTIAL IN WHITE PLANTING SCHEMES, the filigree, silver-white leaves of 'Silver Dust' are the big attraction. A useful, short-growing plant, use it as a colour break between vibrant blocks of summer bedding, or at the front of a border as an attractive edging plant. Tolerant of salt-laden winds, it grows particularly well in mild coastal gardens. In its second summer, loose clusters of mustard-yellow flowers are produced – many gardeners prefer to remove them as they distract from the leaves. Sow the seeds in spring under glass, and grow outdoors in average, well-drained soil.

OTHER VARIETIES 'Alice' (deeply cut, silvery-white leaves); 'Cirrus' (finely toothed or lobed, silver-green to white leaves).

PLANT PROFILE	
HEIGHT	30cm (12in)
SPREAD	30cm (12in)
SITE	Full sun
SOIL	Average, free-draining
HARDINESS	Frost hardy
FLOWERING	Summer

Senecio elegans

A REMARKABLY UNFUSSY PLANT, *S. elegans* grows in just about any soil if given plenty of sun. It has an upright habit with branching stems of jagged-edged, deep green leaves. In summer it produces flat sprays of yellow-eyed flowers which often have an outer ring of purple and occasionally white petals. Use it to fill gaps in cottage-garden borders. Sow the seeds in spring in pots on a windowsill or in a greenhouse, and grow outdoors in average, free-draining soil.

OTHER VARIETY *S. cineraria* (felted, silver-grey leaves, with mustard-yellow flowers).

PLANT PROFILE
HEIGHT 60cm (24in)
SPREAD 35cm (14in)
SITE Full sun
SOIL Average, free-draining
HARDINESS Frost hardy
FLOWERING Summer

S | *Setaria italica* Italian millet

AN EXCELLENT MULTIPURPOSE ANNUAL GRASS, Italian millet (also known as Foxtail millet because it so closely resembles a fox's tail) is perfect for adding height in the garden. From late summer, its creamy-brown, spike-like flowerheads droop down in clusters above the long, thin, narrow leaves. These are followed by golden-yellow, lobed seedheads which are good in dried-flower arrangements – you'll have to be quick with the scissors because they are a favourite with garden birds. Sow the seeds in spring where plants are to flower. Originally from warm, temperate Asia, this grass should be grown in light, free-draining, fertile soil.

PLANT PROFILE

HEIGHT 1.5m (5ft)

SPREAD 1m (3ft)

SITE Sun

SOIL Light, fertile, free-draining

HARDINESS Half hardy

FLOWERING Late summer to autumn

Silene coeli-rosa 'Rose Angel'

S

EQUALLY GOOD AS A CUT FLOWER or for making a low-key border display, 'Rose Angel' produces its magenta flowers over a long period from summer. Mix its seeds with lavender-blue 'Blue Angel' for added interest and sow them in spring or autumn where plants are to flower in neutral to slightly alkaline, average, free-draining soil. To bring flowering forward a few weeks to late spring, sow the seeds at the end of summer in pots in a conservatory. Grow seedlings over winter, ready to plant out the following spring.

OTHER VARIETIES Angel Series (flowers in two soft colours); 'Royal Celebration' (flowers in mixed colours, including red, white and pastel).

PLANT PROFILE
HEIGHT 50cm (20in)
SPREAD 15cm (6in)
SITE Full sun or light dappled shade
SOIL Neutral to slightly alkaline, average, free-draining
HARDINESS Fully hardy
FLOWERING Summer

EDIBLE LEAVES

Also known as the milk thistle, the whole of this plant is edible and said to aid digestion. Its leaves and seeds have even been used to treat the liver.

S

Silybum marianum Blessed Mary's thistle

BLESSED MARY'S THISTLE is one of those rare biennials that is far more impressive in its first year than its second. In year one it produces spiny, glossy, dark green leaves with white veins and marbled patterning. In year two it produces slightly disappointing thistle-like, slightly scented flowers. However, it is an ideal plant for a cottage garden and it also makes a useful filler in a mixed border. Sow the seeds in late spring or early summer where plants are to flower, in poor to average, free-draining soil. The plant will die if it stands in heavy, wet soil over winter. Once established it will readily self-seed – remove unwanted seedlings before the leaves develop their sharp spines.

PLANT PROFILE

HEIGHT 1.5m (5ft)

SPREAD 90cm (36in)

SITE Full sun

SOIL Poor to average, free-draining

HARDINESS Fully hardy

FLOWERING Summer to autumn

Smyrnium perfoliatum Perfoliate Alexanders

LIME-GREEN LEAVES are the key feature of *S. perfoliatum*; its tiny flowers are rather insignificant. A slow grower with erratic germination, you may have to wait until the third year for the plant to really take off. It's worth waiting for, though, as it forms impressive patches of intense colour in the border. Once it becomes established in the garden, the fact that it promptly dies after flowering doesn't matter as it readily sets seed, providing a fresh supply of plants. Take care not to mistake the seedlings for weeds. Sow the seeds in spring in pots in a cold frame, or sow *in situ* in autumn or late spring in average, moist but well-drained soil. perfoliate Alexanders naturalize well in grass and are ideal in woodland or wild gardens.

PLANT PROFILE

HEIGHT 1.5m (5ft)

SPREAD 60cm (24in)

SITE Full sun to partial shade

SOIL Average, moist but free-draining

HARDINESS Fully hardy

FLOWERING Late spring

S

S

Solanum pseudocapsicum 'Red Giant' Christmas cherry

A SHORT, SHRUBBY EVERGREEN, it bears bright red, orange or yellow berries. Usually sold as a winter houseplant, the Christmas cherry also grows well as an annual in a summer border. 'Red Giant' has orange-red fruit over 2.5cm (1in) wide. Sow the seeds in spring under glass, and grow outdoors in moist but well-drained, neutral to slightly alkaline soil. To encourage a good crop of berries, give a liquid tomato feed every two to three weeks when in full growth. Grow pot plants in John Innes No. 2 compost and use an all-purpose liquid feed once a month in addition to the tomato feed. The berries are toxic and should be kept away from children.

OTHER VARIETY 'Cherry Jubilee' (white, yellow or orange fruit).

PLANT PROFILE	
HEIGHT 45cm (18in)	
SPREAD 45cm (18in)	
SITE Full sun	
SOIL Average, moist but free-draining	
HARDINESS Min 5°C (41°F)	
FLOWERING Summer	

Solenopsis axillaris

A SHORT AND DELICATE-LOOKING PLANT for the front of the border, *S. axillaris* produces five-petalled, star-shaped, pale to deep blue flowers in great abundance. They stand out well against the woody stems of dark green narrow leaves. It is a tender plant and won't survive outside in a cold snap – pot plants up in early autumn to overwinter them in a warm greenhouse or conservatory, ready for planting out the following year after the last frost. Bringing plants into the warm should guarantee a few extra weeks of late-season flowers. Deadhead regularly. Sow the seeds in spring in pots on a warm, sunny windowsill or in a greenhouse, and grow outside in average, free-draining soil in full sun.

PLANT PROFILE

HEIGHT 30cm (12in)

SPREAD 30cm (12in)

SITE Full sun

SOIL Average, free-draining

HARDINESS Min 7°C (45°F)

FLOWERING Spring to late autumn

S

Solenostemon scutellarioides Wizard Series Flame nettle

A CULTIVAR OF TROPICAL AND ASIAN PLANTS, Wizard Series is grown not for its flowers but for its foliage colours which can be red, pink, black, and white, usually with a contrasting coloured leaf margin. The insignificant tiny blue or white flowers may appear at any time and are best removed immediately to maintain foliage colour. Sow the seeds in early spring under glass (sprinkle them on top of damp compost but don't cover them over), and grow outdoors in moist but free-draining soil that has been enriched with well-rotted organic matter. The flame nettle also makes an excellent houseplant.

OTHER VARIETY 'Pineapple Beauty' (yellow-green leaves that turn gold, with brown-purple markings).

PLANT PROFILE

HEIGHT 20cm (8in)

SPREAD 20cm (8in)

SITE Full sun or partial shade

SOIL Fertile, moist but free-draining

HARDINESS Min 4°C (39°F)

FLOWERING Summer onwards

Sorghum bicolor Great millet

S

THIS GIANT PLANT LOOKS FABULOUS when grown in tropical-themed borders where its leafy growth and rich green colours will add drama and excitement. Its narrow, waxy leaves reach nearly a metre long (36in) and in the tropics the plant can top 6m (20ft); in colder climes it usually stops at 3m (10ft). The dense, branching clusters of flowers add a quirky touch of pink, purple or pale green. When they ripen, the seedheads look good in dried flower arrangements; spare a few for the birds because the seeds are also a valuable winter food. Sow the seeds in early spring in pots on a sunny windowsill or in a heated greenhouse, and grow outdoors in free-draining, fertile soil.

PLANT PROFILE	
HEIGHT 3m (10ft)	
SPREAD 60cm (24in)	
SITE Sun	
SOIL Fertile, free-draining	
HARDINESS Half hardy	
FLOWERING Summer	

Spraguea umbellata

KNOWN AS PUSSY PAWS in North America, *S. umbellata* is a diminutive plant that is perfect for rock and gravel gardens, as well as the tops of dry-stone walls. The plant forms a ground-hugging rosette of slightly fleshy leaves and short-stemmed sprays of tiny pink flowers appear all summer long. Sow the seeds in spring in pots on a warm windowsill or in a heated greenhouse, and grow outdoors in light, sandy, very free-draining soil. Excellent drainage is the key to success as plants will quickly die if their roots are left sitting in damp soil.

PLANT PROFILE	
HEIGHT 15cm (6in)	
SPREAD 15cm (6in)	
SITE Full sun	
SOIL Light, sandy, very free-draining	
HARDINESS Half hardy	
FLOWERING Summer	

Sutera cordata 'Snowflake'

S

The fragile-looking, attractive star-shaped flowers of this trailing plant swell and fall over the sides of garden containers and hanging baskets. Although they are small – under 2.5cm (1in) – they are produced in great profusion. The leaves are a perfect match, being equally delicate with slightly wavy margins. The most common flower colour is lavender-white, but the pure white flowers of 'Snowflake' are outstanding. Sow the seeds in spring at a temperature of 13–18°C (55–64°F), or divide established plants in spring. Grow outdoors in well-drained, fertile soil. This plant is also sold under its former name of *Bacopa* 'Snowflake'.

PLANT PROFILE
HEIGHT 15cm (6in)
SPREAD Indefinite
SITE Full sun
SOIL Fertile, free-draining
HARDINESS Frost hardy
FLOWERING Summer to autumn

T | *Tagetes* 'Honeycomb' French marigold

A SPLENDID, DWARF-CRESTED FRENCH MARIGOLD, 'Honeycomb' has fully double flowers – about 5cm (2in) wide – in deep, fiery red with an edging of rich orange. Developed from *T. patula*, like all French marigolds, 'Honeycomb' has hairless, purple-tinged stems and deeply cut leaves. Sow the seeds in early spring under glass, or in late spring where plants are to flower in average, free-draining soil. Regular deadheading will help prolong flowering.

OTHER VARIETY Aurora Series (light to golden yellow, orange, or mahogany-red flowers, with some unusual bicolours).

PLANT PROFILE
HEIGHT 25cm (10in)
SPREAD 25cm (10in)
SITE Full sun
SOIL Average, free-draining
HARDINESS Half hardy
FLOWERING Late spring to early autumn

Tagetes 'Lemon Gem' Signet marigold

T

FEW PEOPLE HAVE HEARD of the small, bushy, free-flowering signet
marigolds, but only because they are not marketed as competitively
as other types. Yet they are just as good, generally growing to about
30–35cm (12–14in) high. Among the other members of the Gem
Series are 'Little Gem' which is slightly shorter than the lemon-
yellow 'Lemon Gem'. 'Tangerine Gem' is a lovely deep orange. Sow
the seeds in early spring in pots on a windowsill or in a greenhouse,
or sow *in situ* in late spring in average, free-draining soil. Removing
blooms as soon as they fade will prolong flowering.

OTHER VARIETY 'Starfire' (yellow, golden yellow, and red flowers,
with some bicolours).

PLANT PROFILE
HEIGHT 23cm (9in)
SPREAD 40cm (16in)
SITE Full sun
SOIL Average, free-draining
HARDINESS Half hardy
FLOWERING Late spring to early autumn

Planted next to tomatoes, this marigold is said to keep away whitefly. It may also prevent eelworms damaging roses, tulips and potatoes.

T *Tagetes* 'Naughty Marietta' French marigold

SMALLER THAN THE AFRICAN TYPES, French marigolds are typically about 15–35cm (6–14in) high. 'Naughty Marietta', however, is slightly taller, with rich maroon-red markings radiating out from the centre of the flower. At 15cm (6in), the relatively short Boy Series is another good choice, with double crested flowers in a range of colours, including shades of yellow and orange. Or try 'Tiger Eyes' which has red petals and gold centres. Sow the seeds in early spring under glass, or *in situ* in late spring in average, free-draining soil. Deadheading will prolong flowering.

OTHER VARIETY Hero Series (yellow, golden yellow, orange, red, or mahogany flowers, with crested yellow centres).

PLANT PROFILE

HEIGHT 30–40cm (12–16in)

SPREAD 30cm (12in)

SITE Full sun

SOIL Average, free-draining

HARDINESS Half hardy

FLOWERING Late spring to early autumn

Tagetes 'Vanilla' African marigold

T

THE UPRIGHT, AFRICAN MARIGOLD has pompon-like flowers that are much larger than those of the French marigold. Many make good border plants, growing as tall as 90cm (36in); but some, like 'Vanilla', are much shorter and just the right height for an edging plant. 'Vanilla' is liberally dotted with small, creamy-white flowers, and if you deadhead the plants regularly you will encourage the production of blooms throughout the summer. Sow the seeds in early spring under glass, or in late spring where they are to flower, in average, free-draining soil.

OTHER VARIETY Antigua Series (orange, lemon-yellow, golden yellow or primrose-yellow flowers).

PLANT PROFILE

HEIGHT 35cm (14in)

SPREAD 45cm (18in)

SITE Full sun

SOIL Average, free-draining

HARDINESS Half hardy

FLOWERING Late spring to early autumn

T

Tanacetum haradjanii

COMPACT ENOUGH FOR A ROCK GARDEN, this evergreen perennial can be grown from seed as part of a summer display. The ornamental leaves are a bright silver-grey and are the plant's main attraction, although in late summer there is the bonus of yellow daisy-like flowers. The best time to sow the seeds is in summer, overwintering plants in a frost-free greenhouse, ready to plant out the following year in early summer. A damp root run will quickly kill the plant, and it should be grown in free-draining, preferably sandy, soil.

PLANT PROFILE

HEIGHT 15cm (6in)

SPREAD 20cm (8in)

SITE Full sun

SOIL Free-draining, preferably sandy

HARDINESS Fully hardy

FLOWERING Late summer

Feverfew's bitter-tasting leaves are said to reduce inflammation and act as a mild sedative. It has also been used to treat migraines and arthritis.

Tanacetum parthenium 'Golden Moss' Feverfew

A DWARF, SHRUBBY, CARPET-FORMING PLANT, 'Golden Moss' has aromatic, moss-like, golden leaves and tiny, white, daisy-like flowers. Some gardeners prefer to remove the flowers so that they don't detract from the beautiful leaves. 'Golden Moss' looks good grown to the front of a herb garden. Sow the seeds in summer, keeping plants in a frost-free greenhouse over winter and planting them out the following year in early summer. Grow in free-draining, preferably sandy soil. It is a short-lived plant but, once established, it will self-seed freely.

OTHER VARIETIES 'Butterball' (double yellow flowers); 'Snowball' (ivory-white flowers).

PLANT PROFILE

HEIGHT 10cm (4in)

SPREAD 30cm (12in)

SITE Full sun

SOIL Free-draining, preferably sandy

HARDINESS Fully hardy

FLOWERING Summer

T *Tanacetum parthenium* 'Tom Thumb White Stars' Feverfew

THE PARTHENIUM TANACETUMS (otherwise known as feverfew tanacetums) tend to be short-lived, bushy plants with aromatic foliage. Their daisy-like flowers are produced in summer and look especially good as edging for the front of borders and paths. 'Tom Thumb White Stars' has attractive white, double pompon blooms. Sow the seeds in summer, keeping plants in a frost-free greenhouse over winter and waiting until early summer the following year before planting them out. Grow in free-draining, preferably sandy soil.

OTHER VARIETY 'Butterball' (double yellow flowerheads).

PLANT PROFILE

HEIGHT 23cm (9in)

SPREAD 23cm (9in)

SITE Full sun

SOIL Free-draining, preferably sandy

HARDINESS Fully hardy

FLOWERING Summer

Tanacetum ptarmiciflorum

T

PLANT PROFILE

TOO TENDER TO BE GROWN as a perennial in north-west Europe, *T. ptarmiciflorum* is usually treated as an annual. Like most tanacetums, it is highly prized for its ornamental, pale silver leaves which are about 10cm (4in) long. Used with bolder coloured flowers it makes a startling contrast. Sow the seeds in summer, keeping plants in a frost-free greenhouse over winter and planting them out the following year in early summer. Thereafter, cuttings can be taken in early summer, again for planting out the following year in summer. Grow this as you would other tanacetums, in free-draining, preferably sandy soil.

HEIGHT 60cm (24in)

SPREAD 40cm (16in)

SITE Full sun

SOIL Free-draining, preferably sandy

HARDINESS Half hardy

FLOWERING Late summer

T | *Tanacetum vulgare* 'Silver Lace' Common tansy

VIGOROUS AND QUICK SPREADING, this deciduous perennial is usually grown as an annual in summer schemes. It is prized for its finely divided, silver-variegated leaves which grow to about 15cm (6in) long. The variegation is strong at the start of summer but by the end of the season the leaves are entirely green. Shearing them off as the variegation starts to fade promotes a second crop of silvery leaves, but you will sacrifice the attractive sprays of bright yellow, button-shaped flowers. Sow the seeds in summer, overwintering plants in a frost-free greenhouse. Plant them out the following year in early summer in free-draining, preferably sandy soil.

OTHER VARIETY *T. vulgare* (button-shaped, bright yellow flowers).

PLANT PROFILE	
HEIGHT 60cm (24in)	
SPREAD 45cm (18in)	
SITE Full sun	
SOIL Free-draining, preferably sandy	
HARDINESS Fully hardy	
FLOWERING Summer	

Thunbergia alata Black-eyed Susan

T

THIS ANNUAL CLIMBER FROM TROPICAL AFRICA is easy to grow and will quickly shoot up, twining over shrubs and through other climbers. Dot plants around the garden so you have plenty of opportunity to appreciate the colourful yellow or orange flowers with their velvety-black eyes. *T. alata* can also be grown as a conservatory plant and, if the temperature is kept above 10°C (50°F), it will flower for most of the year. Sow the seeds in spring under glass, and plant outdoors in average, moist but free-draining soil.

OTHER VARIETY *T. gregorii* (clear orange flowers).

PLANT PROFILE

HEIGHT 2m (6ft)

SITE Full sun

SOIL Average, moist but free-draining

HARDINESS Min 7–10°C (45–50°F)

FLOWERING Summer to autumn

T | *Thymophylla tenuiloba* Golden fleece

GOLDEN FLEECE DESERVES GREATER POPULARITY. Its finely divided, aromatic leaves and scores of daisy-like flowers (which are good for cutting), give it a definite edge over similar plants, yet it is rarely seen growing in the garden. It may prove difficult to track down but it is a wonderful plant for hanging baskets, containers, rockeries, and for edging borders and pathways. When its pretty flowers start to fade, snip them off and replacements will soon appear. Sow the seeds in mid-spring under glass, or in mid- to late spring where plants are to flower in average, free-draining soil. Once established, golden fleece is a prolific self-seeder.

PLANT PROFILE

HEIGHT 30cm (12in)

SPREAD 30cm (12in)

SITE Full sun

SOIL Average, free-draining

HARDINESS Frost hardy

FLOWERING Spring to summer

Tithonia rotundifolia 'Torch' **Mexican sunflower**

T

MEXICAN SUNFLOWERS WILL PERK UP a late-summer garden that is starting to look bare and bedraggled. It is a tough, quick-growing, branching annual with showy, bright round flowers – about 8cm (3in) wide – with prominent eyes. Shelter plants from strong winds, and stake them securely so that the flowers don't flop and hide their faces. Water well during dry spells and, before the stems have had a chance to toughen up, keep an eye out for slugs. Sow the seeds in mid- to late spring under glass, or in late spring where plants are to flower, and grow in free-draining, average soil.

OTHER VARIETIES 'Goldfinger' (compact, shorter growing, vivid, rich orange flowers); 'Sundance' (bright orange flowers).

PLANT PROFILE

HEIGHT 2m (6ft)

SPREAD 30cm (12in)

SITE Full sun

SOIL Average, free-draining

HARDINESS Half hardy

FLOWERING Late summer to autumn

T | *Tolpis barbata*

EASY GOING AND VERY SUMMERY, *T. barbata* is a gentle, unassuming, cottage-garden annual that is perfect for the front of the border. The butter yellow flowers, with their fringed petals and handsome dark maroon eye, appear in clusters on top of virtually bare, branching stems. Regular deadheading will keep the display going strong over a long period, from spring right through the summer. The long-stemmed flowers make first-rate cut flowers. Sow the seeds in mid-spring where plants are to flower, in free-draining, average soil.

PLANT PROFILE

HEIGHT 60cm (24in)

SPREAD 30cm (12in)

SITE Full sun

SOIL Average, free-draining

HARDINESS Fully hardy

FLOWERING Spring to summer

Torenia fournieri Clown Series Wishbone flower

T

A LOVELY ANNUAL FOR SUMMER BEDDING with subtle and intriguing patterning on its orchid-like flowers. The Clown Series comes in a palette of soft pinks, purples, lavender-blue shades, and crisp white. As well as using it in the border, enjoy it as a summer-flowering house plant or cool-greenhouse plant. Sow the seeds in mid-spring under glass, and grow in fertile, moist but free-draining soil. Unusually for an annual, it prefers partial shade rather than full sun.

OTHER VARIETIES *T. fournieri* (slightly taller, dark purple, lilac-purple flowers with yellow throats); Panda Series (compact, shorter-growing, white, pink, purple or lavender-blue flowers).

PLANT PROFILE
HEIGHT 25cm (10in)
SPREAD 23cm (9in)
SITE Partial shade
SOIL Fertile, moist but free-draining
HARDINESS Min 5°C (41°F)
FLOWERING Summer

T

Trachelium caeruleum Blue throatwort

THIS UPRIGHT ANNUAL DESERVES to be much more widely grown. It produces clusters of lightly scented, deep violet-blue or white flowers on top of red-flushed stems. The lance-shaped, mid-green leaves are also attractive and grow up to 8cm (3in) long. The best spot for blue throatwort is towards the back of a border, but don't plant it out of reach because you may like to cut the flowers to bring indoors. Sow the seeds in early spring under glass, or in late spring where plants are to flower. Grow in free-draining, average soil where there is shade around midday.

PLANT PROFILE

HEIGHT 1.2m (4ft)

SPREAD 30cm (12in)

SITE Full sun with some midday shade

SOIL Average, free-draining

HARDINESS Half hardy

FLOWERING Summer

COLOURFUL SALADS

The leaves and flowers of nasturtiums can be used fresh in salads, while the large seeds can be pickled. The whole plant is often used in cosmetics.

Tropaeolum majus 'Empress of India' Nasturtium

T

SHORT, BUSHY AND FREE-FLOWERING NASTURTIUMS have been a big hit in cottage gardens for years. For maximum impact for the front of a border, choose the rich scarlet flowers of 'Empress of India': either group plants together for a big display, or wander round the garden with a packet of seeds, sowing them wherever there are gaps needing a shot of hot colour. If you have a planting of bamboos with yellow or orange canes, grow scarlet 'Empress of India' in front for a bright contrast. Sow the seeds in early spring under glass, or late spring where plants are to flower. Grow in average to poor, moist but free-draining soil.

OTHER VARIETY 'Hermine Grasshof' (double, bright red flowers).

PLANT PROFILE

HEIGHT 30cm (12in)

SPREAD 45cm (18in)

SITE Full sun

SOIL Average to poor, moist but free-draining

HARDINESS Half hardy

FLOWERING Summer to autumn

T

Tropaeolum peregrinum Canary creeper

CANARY CREEPER IS A VIGOROUS CLIMBER that can shoot up to an astounding 4m (12ft) over the summer. It has three main attractions. The first is its summer-long display of flashy, bright yellow flowers. Second, the flowers are very distinctive – from a distance they look like exotic butterflies. Third, if given the right support, the growth will form a great mound of bright green foliage. *T. peregrinum* can be grown as a summer screen, but it is only suitable for informal or cottage gardens because its growth habit is far from tidy. Sow the seeds in early spring under glass, or *in situ* in late spring in moist but free-draining, average soil.

PLANT PROFILE

HEIGHT 4m (12ft)

SITE Full sun

SOIL Average, moist but free-draining

HARDINESS Min 3°C (37°F)

FLOWERING Summer to autumn

Tropaeolum Whirlybird Series

A COTTAGE-GARDEN FAVOURITE, the Whirlybird Series puts on a good show of large, open-faced, single to semi-double flowers in shades of cream, red, pink, yellow, and orange. They are held well above a vigorous mound of light green leaves. Given plenty of sun, the Whirlybird Series makes faultless summer bedding, whether for the front of borders, between perennials, on sunny, dry banks, or in containers or hanging baskets. Always have a couple of packets of seeds to hand because there are often gaps to be filled. Sow the seeds in early spring under glass, or in late spring where plants are to flower. Grow in average to poor, moist but free-draining soil.

OTHER VARIETY 'Whirlybird Cream' (creamy-yellow flowers).

PLANT PROFILE
HEIGHT 25cm (10in)
SPREAD 35cm (14in)
SITE Full sun
SOIL Average to poor, moist but free-draining
HARDINESS Half hardy
FLOWERING Early summer to autumn

T

V *Verbascum lychnitis* White mullein

BEST GROWN IN DRIFTS in wildflower or cottage gardens, white mullein has tall, thin, airy branching spires of whitish-yellow flowers that from a distance seem to float in mid air. The plant's mid-green leaves (white underneath) appear towards the base of the plant. This tall verbascum is a subtle alternative to the more imposing, brightly coloured *V. olympicum*. Sow the seeds in autumn under glass; plants will flower the following year. Grow in poor, alkaline, free-draining soil.

OTHER VARIETY *V. arcturus* (lance-shaped, downy, grey-green leaves, saucer-shaped yellow flowers).

PLANT PROFILE
HEIGHT 1.5m (5ft)
SPREAD 60cm (24in)
SITE Full sun
SOIL Alkaline, poor, free-draining
HARDINESS Fully hardy
FLOWERING Summer

Verbascum olympicum

V

TALL AND POWERFULLY UPRIGHT, *V. olympicum* is one of the great sights of summer. It has enormous, greyish–white, felted leaves that can grow up to 60cm (24in) long, and small, yellow, saucer-shaped flowers that appear on branching, candelabra-like stems. Plant *V. olympicum* where it can be seen in its full glory; don't tuck it away at the back of a border. Sow the seeds in late spring or early summer in a cold frame, and plant out in poor, alkaline, free-draining soil. The plant won't flower until its second or third summer.

OTHER VARIETY *V. bombyciferum* (pale yellow, saucer-shaped flowers, white, woolly leaves).

PLANT PROFILE

HEIGHT 2m (6ft)

SPREAD 60cm (24in)

SITE Full sun

SOIL Alkaline, poor, free-draining

HARDINESS Fully hardy

FLOWERING Spring to summer

V

Verbascum phoeniceum 'Flush of White' Mullein

'FLUSH OF WHITE' IS A DELICATE VERBASCUM, with pure white, saucer-shaped flowers. These are massed around slender spikes which rise above a ground-hugging rosette of scalloped-edged, dark green leaves. The summer flowers are followed by attractive seed pods. Sow the seeds in early spring under glass, and plant out in average, free-draining soil. The plants will flower in their first year.

OTHER VARIETY *V. phoeniceum* (saucer-shaped, white, pink or violet to dark purple flowers).

PLANT PROFILE

HEIGHT 75cm (30in)

SPREAD 45cm (18in)

SITE Sun

SOIL Average, free-draining

HARDINESS Fully hardy

FLOWERING Summer

SKIN SOOTHER

This plant's honey-scented flowers are said to soften the skin and are often used to reduce eczema inflammation, help heal wounds and treat coughs.

Verbascum thapsus Aaron's rod

V

A FUN, EYE-CATCHING BIENNIAL, sow the seeds of Aaron's rod (also known as great mullein) in one year and in the next it will send up a single, woolly, sometimes branched stem of yellow, saucer-shaped flowers. The plant adds plenty of impact to any border needing a lift. The height of *V. thapsus* makes it tempting to place it to the back of a border, but it is best appreciated at the front or in the middle surrounded by low plants. Sow the seeds in late spring or early summer in a cold frame; if sown under glass in spring it may flower that summer. Grow in poor, alkaline, free-draining soil.

OTHER VARIETY *V. densiflorum* (saucer-shaped, bright yellow, sometimes white flowers).

PLANT PROFILE

HEIGHT 2m (6ft)

SPREAD 45cm (18in)

SITE Full sun

SOIL Alkaline, free-draining

HARDINESS Fully hardy

FLOWERING Summer

V | *Verbena* 'Temari'

THE TEMARI SERIES OF VERBENAS offers both toughness and lots of colour – bright pink, soft pink and hot pink, as well as burgundy, are among the most popular shades available. The bicolour flowers of 'Temari' are a striking combination pink-purple and white and appear on top of long stems above dark green foliage. Sow the seeds in autumn or early spring under glass, at a temperature of 18–21°C (64–70°F). Grow outdoors in average, moist but free-draining soil.

OTHER VARIETIES 'Silver Anne' (sweetly scented, bright pink flowers that fade to silver-white); 'Sissinghurst' (magenta-pink flowers).

PLANT PROFILE

HEIGHT 70cm (28in)

SPREAD 60cm (24in)

SITE Sun

SOIL Average, moist but free-draining

HARDINESS Fully hardy

FLOWERING Summer to autumn

Viola x *wittrockiana* 'Imperial Antique Shades' Pansy

THE SOFT, PALE ORANGE TO PALE APRICOT FLOWERS of the 'Imperial Antique Shades' put on a good show in containers and windowboxes. And unlike most of the large-flowered but compact Imperial Series, the petals of this cultivar are unmarked. Its a result of cross breeding *V. altaica*, *V. cornuta*, *V. lutea* and *V. tricolor*, the x wittrockiana cultivars are usually much larger and more robust than their parents. Sow the seeds in early spring under glass, or in summer where plants are to flower the following winter. Plant out in fertile, moist but free-draining soil.

OTHER VARIETY Bingo Series (large flowers, produced in winter and spring, in a broad colour range, some with darker markings).

PLANT PROFILE
HEIGHT 23cm (9in)
SPREAD 25cm (10in)
SITE Full sun or partial shade
SOIL Fertile, moist but free-draining
HARDINESS Fully hardy
FLOWERING Winter to early spring

X | *Xeranthemum annuum*

CUT THE DELICATE, DAISY-LIKE FLOWERS of *X. annuum* before they
have fully opened and hang them upside down in a cool, dark, well–
ventilated place to dry. These single to double flowers, produced
from summer to autumn, come in a wide range of colours, including
white, bright pink, crimson-red, or chocolate-purple. A slender,
upright annual, originally from the steppes and stony banks in the
Mediterranean to south-west Asia, *X. annuum* has woolly, silver-green
leaves on wiry stems that branch from the base of the plant. Sow the
seeds in spring under glass, and grow in average, well-drained soil
in full sun. Provide support on exposed sites.

OTHER VARIETY 'Snow Lady' (single, white flowers).

PLANT PROFILE

HEIGHT 75cm (30in)

SPREAD 45cm (18in)

SITE Full sun

SOIL Average, free-draining

HARDINESS Half hardy

FLOWERING Summer to
autumn

Zinnia elegans Peppermint Stick Series

Z

CONSIDERED GREAT FUN BY SOME and a hideous, mad blotch by others, the bizarre-looking flowers of the Peppermint Stick Series are quite unlike the dahlia-like flowerheads of most zinnias. With pompon-like blooms on sturdy, upright stems, the petals of this series are splashed and striped in a wide range of exuberant colours. Sow the seeds in succession in early spring under glass, or late spring where plants are to flower. Grow in fertile, free-draining soil.

OTHER VARIETIES 'Envy' (semi-double, chartreuse-green flowers); Thumbelina Series (dwarf, single or semi-double, yellow, red, magenta, or pale pink flowers).

PLANT PROFILE
HEIGHT 60cm (24in)
SPREAD 30cm (12in)
SITE Full sun
SOIL Fertile, free-draining
HARDINESS Min 10°C (50°F)
FLOWERING Summer to autumn

The publisher would like to thank the following for their kind permission to reproduce their photographs:

a=above; c=centre; b=below; l=left; r=right t=top;

A-Z Botanical Collection:
46c, 66c, 85c, 100c, 183c, 271c, 277c; Chris Martin Bahr 287tr, 287c; Mowenna Busby 313c; Carol Casselden 233c; Michael R.Chandler 109c; Mrs Pam Collins 49c; Mike Danson 19c, 88c, 202c, 284c; Derrick Ditchburn 244tr, 244c; Robert J.Erwin 159c, 173c; Bob Gibbons 276c; Peter Jackson 132c; K.Jayaram 78c; Malcolm Richards 84c, 104c, 229c; Dan Sams 51c, 106c, 127c, 131c, 141c, 142c, 246c; Roger Standen 130c; Jan Staples 126c; Adrian Thomas 55c, 89c, 110c, 138c, 140c, 243c, 268c; Chris Wheeler 168c
Brian North:
4c
Eric Crichton Photos:
61c, 145c
Mr Fothergill's Seeds:
56c, 56c, 102c
Garden Picture Library:
David Askham 34c; Chris Burrows 289c; John Glover 7r; Juliet Greene 20c; Jerry Pavia 192c; Lorraine Pullin 294c; Howard Rice 90c, 128c, 181c
Garden World Images:
6br, 33c, 63tr, 63c, 64c, 75tr, 75c, 77c, 95c, 97c, 117c, 156c, 171c, 231c, 247c, 252c

Holt Studios International:
Nigel Cattlin 193c; Primrose Peacock 199c
Andrew Lawson:
53c
Natural Image:
Bob Gibbons 79c
Photos Horticultural:
35c, 77c, 80c, 148c, 149c, 162c, 194c, 204c, 228c, 239c, 295c, 304c, 308c
Plant Pictures World Wide:
24c, 27c, 32c, 40c, 97tr, 118c, 129c, 185c, 190c, 248c, 279c, 288c
Suttons Seeds:
184c, 245c, 275c, 312C, 312c
Unwins Seeds Ltd:
86c.

All other images © Dorling Kindersley.

For further information see:
www.dkimages.com

Dorling Kindersley would also like to thank the following:
Helen Fewster and Letitia Luff for their editorial assistance; Michele Clarke for the index; and Archie Clapton in Media Resources.